ZEN DEMYSTIFIED

RAFAEL PINTOS-LÓPEZ

Copyright © 2024 by Rafael PINTOS-LÓPEZ

All rights reserved.

No part of this book may be reproduced in any form or by any electronic or mechanical means, including information storage and retrieval systems, without written permission from the author, except for the use of brief quotations in a book review.

ISBN: 978-0-6458780-4-2

❦ Created with Vellum

CONTENTS

Untitled	vii
Preface	xi
Introduction	xix
1. Human Consciousness	1
2. Language and Culture	16
3. Interest in Eastern mysticism	28
4. Buddhism in India and China	36
5. Japan and Zen	49
6. Cognition, Time and Identity	57
7. Sentience and Self-awareness	66
Conclusion	79
Acknowledgments	103

Dedicated to Jack Kerouac, who dedicated 'The Dharma Bums' to Han Shan.

"Studying texts and stiff meditation can make you lose your Original Mind. A solitary tune by a fisherman, though, can be an invaluable treasure. Dusk rain on the river, the moon peeking in and out of the clouds; Elegant beyond words, he chants his song night after night." -Ikkyu

∽

"If I were to demonstrate the Great Matter in strict keeping with the teaching of the Founders' School, I simply couldn't open my mouth."

-Linji

∽

"The past mind is unattainable, the present mind is unattainable, and the future mind is unattainable"

-Diamond Sutra

∽

"Abiding nowhere, the mind comes forth."

-Diamond Sutra

∽

"Thirty blows if you can't speak, thirty blows if you can."

-Huangbo

∽

"There really isn't much to Huangbo's Buddha-Dharma."

-Linji

~

"If you call this a khakkhara (short staff), you go against reality. If you do not call it a khakkhara, you ignore the fact. Now, what do you want to call this?"

-Shuzan, holding out his short staff.

~

Monk: *"What is the difference between the enlightened and the unenlightened man?"*

Master: *"The unenlightened see a difference, whereas the enlightened do not see such difference"*

~

Jizo: *"Where are you going, 'joza' (senior monk)?"*

Hōgen: *"I'm on a pilgrimage, following the wind."*

Jizo: *"What are you on a pilgrimage for?"*

Hōgen: *"I don't know."*

Jizo: *"Not knowing is most intimate."*

Hōgen was suddenly enlightened.

~

Monk: *"Master, instruct me in Zen"*.

Joshu: *"Have you not had your breakfast?"*

Monk: *"Yes, Master, I have"*.

Joshu: *"Then, go wash your bowls"*.

Vasettha: *"My path is the true path to salvation. It leads to union with Brahma."*

Gautama: *"Has any Brahmin seen Brahma face to face?"*

Vasettha: *"No."*

Gautama: *"If that is so, their path is groundless. It is like a file of blind men, following each other. The first one sees nothing, the middle one sees nothing, and the last one sees nothing. The talk of the Brahmin is empty and vain. Mere words."*

Men ask the way through the clouds,

The cloud way's dark, without a sign.

High summits are of naked rock.

In deep valleys sun never shines.

Behind you green peaks, and in front,

To east the white clouds, and to west –

Want to know where the cloud way lies?

It's there, in the centre of the Void!

Han Shan - *The Cold Mountain*

PREFACE

For a long time, Zen has enjoyed an unparalleled attraction in the West. Few know what it is, though. An aura of mystery surrounds it like a thick fog. Zen Masters and monks do not make it any easier; there is no welcoming mat, no introductory chat forthcoming, no PowerPoint presentation. Come and meditate if you wish, otherwise, you can always stay away. Nobody talks about it, mainly because they are not supposed to. Perhaps I should clarify now that the word "demystified" in the title does not allude to any deception on the part of any Zen founder, master, practitioner, or monk. There is, however, a very clear anti-intellectual strain in Zen, much more than in any other type of Buddhism. There appears to be a kind of obscurantism to it. And of course—as we shall see here—there is a reason for it. Zen is the exact opposite of intellectualism.

~

PREFACE

When I started writing this book, the idea was to convey some Buddhist notions, especially about Zen, to the Western public in a form that would be understandable.

If you have read anything about Zen before borrowing or buying this book—and I bet you have—the idea would sound totally absurd. It would sound a bit like an oxymoron because, according to Zen, there is nothing to understand. What the Masters will tell you is that Zen is not a religion, and it's not a philosophy either: it cannot be transmitted as information, or using language. Meditation practice, way of life... yes, but where does it take you? Do we know what enlightenment is? Do we know what the process involves?

In this instance, I must admit the information I have about Eastern religions, philosophy or ideas is fairly limited. Again, lack of information should not be an impediment. Zen itself, we have been saying, rejects anything to do with logic, or words, and that's what Western explanations are all about. Check out the *'koans'* (which are a kind of riddle with no possible solution) and Buddhist sayings that precede this *Preface* and then decide for yourself if they make any sense at all.

On occasions, this explanation will need to go around Buddhism and Zen and you will realise why. That is not another excuse for my ignorance of the main topic. The way this book will clear the fog around Zen has more to do with an analysis of human consciousness than with religion, philosophy or meditation. Do not worry though, later I will clarify what I mean.

In the pages that follow I will attempt to meet the promise implied in the title. I will guide the reader, to the best of my ability, towards an answer: the reader will reach an understanding of Zen through explanation, something not attempted before, as far as I know.

With all due respect to D.T. Suzuki and the many Zen Masters who have claimed that Zen cannot be understood by means of words, I will try to do exactly that. The reader will not achieve *satori*, but he or she will grasp the logic behind it. He or she will understand how it works and maybe, as a layperson, even profit from its teachings.

This is not a self-help book. As I state above, reading this will not provide instant enlightenment, nor the wellness other authors promise; it will only give you an understanding of what a Western student of Zen may expect, what Zen involves.

The funny thing is that, even if it's not a self-help book, just by explaining how Zen operates, there will be some answers that the reader will be able to apply to his or her daily life. The reader will probably find that the book offers unexpected solutions to some of his or her problems. I do not claim, though, that I can advise anybody on how to lead their lives. The answers found here are Zen answers, not mine.

Like many of the good things in life, I came to understand how Zen works by a stroke of luck. I did not do all the hard work required to attain satori, all the practice, all the meditation, all the years of being a monk. I just stumbled on how the process operates. Probably, the best way to describe this book is that it is like a technical roadmap. It could be used as a plan for the reader to help him or her decide whether they want to start the Zen journey or maybe achieve some other goal.

Better still, when I think about it, this book is like a brochure, or an owner's manual. If you are about to buy a powerful machine, a subscription, or life insurance, but do not quite understand how the thing is actually going to do the work for you, you need someone to tell you whether the machine, the subscription, or the insurance policy will do exactly that. Well, this brochure tells you how much Zen can help you and how it does it.

Zen is like the manufacturer and your machine, or the insurance company; it promises the machine or the policy will work, it says you must have faith that it will. After many years of hard work, concentration and meditation, it will be like a surprise and you'll enjoy it tremendously. It will change your life. Sometimes, enlightenment comes immediately, sometimes after many years of meditation but—they say—it is always sudden. *Satori* is actually a revelation, Zen practitioners tell you.

I, on the other hand—an outsider—believe what they say, the revelation bit and all that, but apart from assuring you that it *does* work, will try to analyse *how* it does it, so that you will understand (the same way I believe I did, with a Western mind). Maybe a Zen master one day will come and tell me it's not like that at all. I doubt it, though. The workings appear quite clear to me. Even though Zen Masters tell you that only blind faith in the process of Zen will take you there, I believe understanding the process beforehand gives you a leg up, especially if you are a Westerner.

The book includes an *Introduction*, a chapter on *Human Consciousness*, and one on *Language and Culture*. They may appear totally unrelated at first, but they are vital to comprehending the concepts that follow. Then come two more chapters that are really optional reading: *Interest in Eastern Mysticism* and *Buddhism in India and China*. They are mainly historical but include information you might find interesting, and/or helpful. What comes after these: *Japan and Zen, Cognition, Time and Identity, Sentience and Self-awareness* and the *Conclusion,* are the segments that, I believe, will finally clarify the workings of Zen in the mind of the reader.

In general, it is true, no amount of reading, no amount of information—I have discovered—would bring the reader even close to *satori*, exactly the opposite. In the end, and in a very Zen way, you will have to figure it out by yourself. Only experience will work. Zen is basically a mystical practice (experience if you like). Here, I agree with the Masters. Again, this apparent contradiction will have to be explained. You will see why.

In the twentieth century, many young people were attracted to the idea of Buddhism and especially of Zen. Naïvely, many (and I include myself among them) thought that books would show them the way to enlightenment. But books—

lovely as they are—could not show, could not demonstrate, they could only impart information.

The path to Zen is a difficult one: the Japanese have a language and a culture that are unlike any European language and culture. There are many differences with the West, but let's say that the main one resides in the manner in which Judaism and Christianity attempted to explain human consciousness, a long time ago, and how it developed from there, passing through the Renaissance and the Reformation. The Western vision of how human consciousness operates is a highly individualistic one. Also, it is partly grounded on a dichotomy: subject/object which is—in many ways—misleading.

Objective reality has been a very useful concept that ultimately allowed the West to develop science and technology. Unfortunately, when it comes to comprehending consciousness, it becomes an impediment. In this case, neuroscience, for instance, will need to understand what quantum physics has already understood. There are no separate realities for the individual and his or her circumstances. Observer and observed are one and the same.

Sometimes, when a jet plane transitions from subsonic to supersonic speed, control reversal becomes necessary. A rare aerodynamic phenomenon makes it essential for the pilot to do exactly the opposite of what he or she would do in subsonic conditions. Sometime in the future, Western science and philosophy will learn that consciousness has no correlates in the individual brain.

Experience, sentience, just occurs. It is a 'fundamental'. How it occurs—or whether Western science will work it out—is not something we want to discuss here. (I am sure, however, that eventually neuroscience will find that it is impossible to study the emergence of human consciousness departing from the individual brain). The point is they will need to reverse the controls. Among other things, Zen shows how human consciousness operates, you will see.

This book is grounded on the assumption that human consciousness is layered, that it includes two integrated but discrete components: sentience (the biological component), and cognition (the cultural, meta-evolutionary component), and—further—, that 'time' is a human construct. I am convinced that those ideas are correct, and Buddhism in general aligns with them.

Writing about human consciousness, I came to the realisation that only within cognition (the cultural component) it is possible to apply the notion of an objective reality—which involves the separation subject/object. The same goes for 'time'. It works only within the intellect. That principle came to me as a joyful epiphany. Not quite *satori*, but it led me to understand how it works. It was like the vision of a still-to-be-painted watercolour in all its ideal simplicity and luminosity.

Sentience, on the other hand, has no separation between subject and object, nor does it have time. As stated before, quantum physics has recently reached that conclusion: observer and observed are one and the same. That is the principle of Zen. Reality is oneness.

The discovery was that some schools of Buddhism, like Zen, reject logic because cognition (which includes logic) is the origin of human suffering. Eastern ideas, as stated, align with the theory of a layered consciousness and—in their own way—clarify many things, especially to do with the pervasiveness of thought and how bad that can be for humans.

The idea that followed the first realisation—which was extremely interesting—was that, if meditation could separate the components of human consciousness, which are intertwined, that meant not only that they are discrete, but that their nature is different.

But, enough of stories. Let's see what this book has to say about Zen.

INTRODUCTION

"So far Zen has been discussed from the intellectual point of view, in order to see that it is impossible to comprehend Zen through this channel; in fact, it is not doing justice to Zen to treat it thus philosophically. Zen abhors media, even the intellectual medium; it is primarily and ultimately a discipline and an experience, which is dependent on no explanation; for an explanation wastes time and energy and is never to the point, all that you get out of it is misunderstanding and a twisted view of the thing."

D.T. Suzuki - *An Introduction to Zen Buddhism*

"... we have to keep on dreaming until we abolish the false boundary between what is illusory and what is tangible, until we achieve our aspirations and discover

INTRODUCTION

that the paradise lost was always there, around every corner."

– Julio Cortázar

Semiconductors are used in electronic circuitry. They are basically a physical object with some energy going through it.

Why is a semiconductor called a semiconductor? It is, actually, a material used to conduct current. It is not as conductive as a conductor—which has full conductivity—but it's more conductive than an insulator, which does not allow any current to go through. Silicone is an example of a semiconductor.

Copper is an example of a conductor: electricity flows through it very easily; on the other hand, rubber or glass are examples of insulators; that is, they stop current.

This is absurd. Why is this crazy book explaining semiconductors, when it's supposed to be discussing Zen?

Well, the answer is, because it wants to start by proving that explaining certain concepts is possible. That is an example of something—obscure to most—that can be explained in simple terms. Now you know what a semiconductor is.

There are things that cannot be explained, though. They can only be demonstrated; undoubtedly demonstration is one of the best ways of teaching. But then, demonstration is partly practice.

In general, if you want to read about the theory behind Zen, you will find that there are no explanations. Is there a theory?

INTRODUCTION

There is no theory. This book, however, will attempt to peep behind the practice and find out what lies there. There is a progression that goes roughly like this: experience > expertise > wisdom. This does not tell you much at this stage. Keep on reading.

You will find many other books about Zen, and they will not explain what Zen is. Or maybe they will give you some indication as to what Zen is, but will not explain how it works. They will have pictures showing what monks do, beautiful gardens, and things like the tea ceremony. They will not explain it because it is like trying to explain a colour. Like explaining a sound. Why is it like trying to explain a colour or a sound? We'll get into that similarity a little later. We will not explain the practice, of course, we will explain what's behind it.

If you want to 'explain' how red occurs, you can discuss wavelengths, energy, hues, spectrum. That is possible, but the experience of the colour will not come through with that kind of approach. Imagine a person, blind from birth, trying to understand what you are talking about.

Is there a way to tell how you feel when you are sensory-deprived? Do you feel any different when that happens? You cannot explain it. Well... you can put someone in a dark, soundproof tank full of water and they will find out. Only the experience can tell the person what it feels like.

Or, let's put it in different terms, something even more complex. Suppose you are at the Museum of Modern Art in New York City, and you have *"Starry Night"* by Vincent Van Gogh, in front of you. You are on the phone, wanting to describe, to a friend in Sydney, how the painting makes you

INTRODUCTION

feel. It would be possible for you to talk about the swirling sky, the stars, the little village, and the brushstrokes, or the dark pigments, but you will not be able to explain what you feel in any detail.

Maybe what's happening to you is that, through time and space, you are feeling a special connection with the painter. Maybe you can empathise with Vincent, with his craziness and his depression. Your Australian friend will probably be able to guess a tiny fraction of your direct experience. A description is as close as you can go in the (impossible) transmission of an experience. Or maybe a photo of the painting will help to a point. Who knows?

I will give you another example: you're on holidays, strolling before lunch. You are looking for a restaurant, in the middle of the Ramblas, in Barcelona, when a flashmob plays what appears like an impromptu version of *"Ode to Joy"*. You stop and listen. The glory of European civilisation invades the street; everybody sings; Beethoven and Schiller's genius flows within you; it's a gift that you'll never forget. You record every moment, every note on your telephone. When you play it back at the hotel, it's not quite the same. You'll remember, but the experience will be lost. It was something unique that you cannot revisit any more. Not in its entirety, even if you can reproduce vision and sound.

Second-hand experiences do not exist. Semiconductors can be explained, but experience is unique and ineffable. It is something you yourself (and nobody else) feels. It cannot be repeated, and no descriptions will come even close.

Good teachers have a fantastic way around that problem: parables. Parables are a longer form of metaphor, one that involves concrete examples, they're basically illustrations of what they want to teach. Buddha and Jesus used parables extensively. They knew a parable was closest to a demonstration than to an explanation. And the difference lies in how the idea is transmitted. Their nature is different from that of explanations and/or demonstrations.

A demonstration is close to the real experiential phenomenon. In a parable you are given a simile, a parallel template where you can place the ideas the teacher wants you to focus on, and understand the situation. An explanation requires thought (and language). A demonstration doesn't. A parable lies somewhere in between.

American Indian mothers don't tell their children that fire burns. They allow them to touch the flame. Children learn through experience and never forget.

Currently, neuroscientists are trying to explain human consciousness by finding the correlates of experience in the brain. The search is useless because that spot is only part of it. The experience will not be there. Only the location of neurones and synapses.

This book will attempt to explain to you why words cannot describe or reproduce experience. What the explanation will entail does not include the actual experience, but the process.

Well, let's start by saying that, chronologically, experience came long before language. Experience is the more atavistic component of the way we understand reality. So, there was a time when protohuman individuals, hominins, experienced through their senses but did not need to use language. Experience, then, predates words.

INTRODUCTION

Language is analytical by nature. If you think about it, it normally divides an occurrence into a subject, a verb and an object (yes, it's more complex than that, I know). But if I tell you "The fox jumps over the fence", you understand the idea. The fox just jumps: he undergoes a direct experience.

I repeat, this book will try to analyse the hidden meaning of Zen for you. In this Introduction, it will do it by briefly following the history of the religions and philosophies of both East and West.

At first, this Introduction will appear totally unrelated to Zen. There is a point to it, though. Please bear with me. You'll get there.

From my perspective, religion, philosophy and science are part of the same paradigm. They are all part of the same human quest for knowledge. Following completely different paths, they attempted—and still attempt—to provide answers for the transcendental questions humanity asks. Their answers differ because they occurred, and are still occurring, at different times and within different cultures.

As stated, one of the most important questions we ask ourselves is that of human consciousness. What is it? How do we feel and perceive reality? How do we think? How can we do all that? How do we decide when to act? How do we choose what is right and what is wrong?

That, of course, involves self-awareness; interoception (i.e., how our body feels); and exteroception (how we perceive the reality that surrounds our skin); but it also involves thought, identity; time, etc.

It is an extremely complicated subject; West and East approached it in completely different ways.

The first important answers—at least for the West—came from the Bible, around eight centuries before Christ. In the Bible, the ancient Hebrews compiled all the oral traditions that had been transmitted through countless generations, from parents to children and around campfires.

In the Book of Genesis, both Adam and Eve are created by God before really becoming human (Gen. I: 27-28). At the beginning, they are like all other animals. Then, language is introduced (Gen. II: 20-25). Then comes the Myth of Adam and Eve in Paradise (Gen. III). It is a description of the moment a pair of hominins become human. The creation of humanity as a species. Once Adam speaks, he can name all the animals; after that, both Adam and Eve can think, and what happens in the myth is that—contrary to God's warning—they find out what's right and what's wrong and they can decide what to do (the Tree of Knowledge of Good and Evil).

Unfortunately, it is easier to interpret myths literally. They are an easy-to-understand alternative explanation to what really happened. Those days, Judaism and Christianity did not have the tools to explain, in any other way, how humanity or human consciousness had come to be. Of course, the real process that is described in the Myth of the

Garden of Eden (the introduction of cognition) must have taken thousands of years. Christianity and Judaism choose the literal interpretation. Adam and Eve learn to speak, and think, and judge for themselves, and God then tells them that the consequences would be dire.

The Old Testament (i.e., the *Tanakh*, or Hebrew Bible) explains 'life' by means of a Hebrew word, נפש *("nephesh")*, which has been often translated as "life", or "breath of life", something that God instils in animals. Animals acquire that quality the instant they are born.

The moment an animal exists, it can sense its surroundings and, more often than not, move (although a few primitive animal forms—like the sponge—do not move). Nowadays, we would probably use the term "sentience" to describe the phenomenon.

Even though *"nephesh"* is often translated as "soul" or "breath of life", the Book of Genesis never discusses cognition in humans—as opposed to sentience in animals—by using one specific word. The only description it provides for "*psyche*" is the 'knowledge of good and evil' that the myth mentions.

In any case, the Old Testament describes humanity as something separate from the rest of Creation. God puts Adam in charge of all animals. Not of all *other* animals. Humans are definitely in a separate class. That concept would be adopted by Christianity and would evolve in Western philosophy. There is something subjective (the human mind), and a separate reality that is objective (the rest of reality). Humans can observe, analyse and study anything that is objective.

Humans can think. And we do it from the perspective of a consciousness that is inside the body, looking out.

The New Testament (i.e., Christianity) further emphasised the concept of the separation between human beings and animals. A Greek word, ψυχή ("psyche") probably related to "psykhein", which coincidentally means to breathe, to blow) is used extensively in the Gospels to indicate "soul". According to the Gospels, souls are exclusively human. That word is never used in the Old Testament because it was only introduced as a Christian concept. The Gospels say humans have an individual immortal soul. That is what we now call psyche (same word), which we believe dies with the individual.

According to Christianity, then, when good Christians die, they go to Heaven with God. The Son of God becomes human, dies and resurrects. Any good human who believes in Christianity goes to Heaven, it doesn't matter if they are slaves, prostitutes or kings. Human beings are basically demigods.

Christianity—that commenced as a peripheral sect of Judaism, and whose leaders and followers were mostly illiterate, like the rest of the nation—eventually became the religion of the Roman Empire, and then of the West. If Western countries have anything in common is that they share Judaeo-Christian morals, ethics and philosophy. Understanding how that occurs is easy: there is a common tradition, there is a shared history.

We are not going to enter here into how Saul of Tarsus (aka St Paul) adopted the Greek concept of an immortal soul, as proposed by Plato, and used it as a fundamental element of Christianity, but that is what happened.

The most important philosophical concept derived from Christianity and adopted by the West is that of "objective reality". As we have seen, human beings are above the rest of creation, and can study and understand the universe. They have a separate, subjective, reality inside of them. On that basis, Western scholars developed what we now classify as science and technology. Science can study the universe and establish laws. Science, clearly defined as such, commenced in the West with Newton and, for a long time, remained as a solely Western institution

As explained, the way the West developed has been profoundly influenced by Christianity, which is a mixture of Judaism and Greek thought. The West, in many ways, is the product of Christianity. The individualism built into our culture comes from European languages and from Aristotelian philosophy but also from St Paul, St Augustine and St Thomas Aquinas, who added Greek thought to Jesus' message. This gave Aristotelian philosophy an aura of mysticism, and Christianity an aura of truth. The "self" is central to both. Greek philosophers developed the notion of the individual immortal soul (which later became "mind") and Christianity adopted the immortality of that soul. As we saw, the word they used is the same, "*psyche*". Somehow, the West grew together with Christianity. That growth included the appearance of concepts like objective truth and critical thinking. Science developed naturally out of those two. Objective truth is one of the logical conclusions of Western solipsism. According to it we are separate beings. Our ego is separate from the universe. Therefore, we can study the universe as an

INTRODUCTION

object. An object that can be studied and analysed. Hence, science.

The East, and some currents of Greek thought, like Heraclitus, for instance, found that concept impossible; they treat the subject and the object as one and the same, and everything as dynamic phenomena, everything flows.

During the beginnings of Christianity, the Fathers of the Church persecuted the doctrines they called "heresies."

The process had really begun with the Roman Tetrarchs (the four "emperors"). After some years of co-operation under the Tetrarchs, the Western and Eastern Roman Empires went their separate ways, and ended up not having very friendly relations. The Eastern Empire—Byzantium—had maintained, to some extent, the knowledge of the ancient Greeks.

Invaded by Barbarian tribes, the Western Empire had fallen into what is now called the Dark Ages. Libraries were small and most books were blindly copied by monks and kept in monasteries. The populace and many members of the nobility were illiterate.

Rome and Byzantium—both Christian—had been invaded and threatened even further by Islam. In 1453, Byzantium's capital, Constantinople, finally fell to the onslaught of the Ottoman armies of Sultan Mehmet II. Many Byzantines fled and settled as refugees in the Italian peninsula; Cardinal Bessarion was among them. The Cardinal had amassed a large collection of Greek and Latin manuscripts which he later donated to the Republic of Venice and are now part of St Mark's Library.

INTRODUCTION

Bessarion's donation kickstarted the Renaissance. Florence became Europe's centre of art and learning. Around that time, Johannes Gutenberg had invented the movable-type printing press. Roughly a century later, the Reformation followed. By then, Europe already had universities and scholars.

Driven by curiosity and greed, astrology and alchemy began as forbidden observations and experiments. Secretly, they gave birth to astronomy and chemistry; other, more specialised, scientific disciplines branched out from them. Science then crept slowly out of a nebula of superstition. In its early days, the West developed strangely. It was like a dance in which religion, philosophy, art, and finally science, acted as the four bases of Western DNA, which intertwined to form the double helix of our culture. Newton—an alchemist—would be initiator and reference in this transformation. Descartes—an amateur magician—would become one the greatest philosophers of the West, the father of Substance Dualism.

To summarise the basics of this segment, why is the West not the best place to become enlightened (when enlightenment means something like *nirvana* or *satori*)? Well, there are important differences between East and West. The philosophical grounds on which the cultures are based are diametrically opposed. How is that? As we have seen, Western philosophy is based on the self and an objective separate reality that surrounds the self; in the East, it is quite the opposite, selflessness, where the self is part of reality, and it is also intersubjectively dependent, i.e., the self is defined by its relationships, and relationships are fluid.

INTRODUCTION

The way things have turned out, it is not surprising to discover that what happened in the East was totally different. A civilisation had developed in the Indian subcontinent over several millennia. By twenty-six hundred BCE, the Indus Valley culture had large cities, with tenths of thousands of inhabitants, like Mohenjo-daro and Harappa. That civilisation was coetaneous with other large Asian settlements, basically, those of the Yellow River and the Yangtze.

During the fifth to the fourth centuries BCE, Siddharta Gautama, a Nepalese prince—or so the legend goes—founded a new movement later called Buddhism (from '*boddhi*', or awakening).

The same way Christianity branched out of Judaism, Buddhism was born as a sect in the periphery of Hinduism. Some consider it a religion; some, a philosophy; to some, it's just a way of life. From my perspective, it's all of those and more, depending on the school of Buddhism.

As we were saying, Gautama Buddha thought of life as something dynamic. Life passes. Time passes. Everything is transient. Wanting to cling to something transient as you would something permanent causes unhappiness. In short, he taught the way to let go of impermanent things and situations. The way of detachment.

Pretty much like Jesus became the Christ, two centuries after his death, Gautama was declared the Saviour, the Buddha, the Enlightened One.

INTRODUCTION

A legendary holy man called Bodhidharma took Buddhism from India to the South of China, where it grew. In the North, Confucianism was prevalent. Buddhism developed some common concepts with it. They were both influenced by the teachings of a legendary character, Fu Xi, who had written his *I Ching*—or *Book of Changes*— a book and a divination system. It dates from the tenth century BCE and includes principles and directives for a happy life. It has been described as "a living stream of deep human wisdom". Lao Tzu and Confucius were both familiar with the *I Ching*. Many of these beliefs have coexisted for centuries and have some similarities. Among other things, the *I Ching* teaches about modesty, peace and restraint. It also shows the negative influences of the ego: fear, anxiety, anger, desire, and other undesirable feelings. To this day, Zen Buddhism coexists with Shinto, or Japanese ancestor worship.

From the South of China, Mahayana Buddhism went to Japan, where it underwent transformations until it derived into a type of Buddhism originally called *zazen* (a name derived from the act of meditating cross-legged), which was later shortened to Zen.

HUMAN CONSCIOUSNESS

"Why does the mind habitually deny or resist the Now? Because it cannot function and remain in control without time, which is past and future, so it perceives the timeless Now as threatening. Time and mind are in fact inseparable."

Eckhart Tolle - *The Power of Now*

We have seen that, even though the scribes who compiled the Hebrew Bible touched upon the notion of consciousness, it was Greek thinkers who were the first in the West to ponder the complexities of the human mind. They established the main Western rule of consciousness: the body dies; *psyche*—the soul—which is the exact opposite of the body, does not die. Body and soul have different natures.

St Paul adopted the Greek idea of an individual immortal soul. In the case of Christian thought, that individual soul goes to Heaven (or maybe not). The case is that, according to both, ancient Greeks philosophers and Christians in general, body and soul still are essentially different.

Descartes based his Substance Dualism on the fact that mind and body were completely different: their properties were quite distinct. They both existed but the nature of their existence was dual and opposite. Descartes knew that his mind could think. His body could not think. Both, his body and his mind existed but they were separate entities, they were made of different substances, and had different natures. He established that he existed, i.e., if he could think that he was alive, that meant that he actually was alive. He reached that conclusion using metacognition, which is really thinking about thinking.

Right now, neuroscientists, philosophers and other scholars are trying to determine the point in the brain where neurones generate human experience: the correlates of consciousness. At this moment, when physicalism reigns in academia, their search only includes sentience. How does the body produce sentience? Well, sentience is fundamental and it is shared by all animals and some plants. I will not enter into what 'fundamental' means, maybe we could use the word primeval, or something that exists from the beginning. Let's say this is not the place to try and explain it. We would be digressing a lot.

Having said that, it is true that academia is currently convinced that evolutionary biology and physicalism constitute the right approach to consciousness, but we need to mention that, after decades of failures with that approach, there are signs of rebelliousness in the study of the mind. Some psychologists now consider that physicalism fails to account for social thought and behaviour (yes!). That is, they believe there is a world beyond the individual and the brain. They believe you cannot ignore social consciousness. One of the important implications of this new type of model is that it emphasises interconnectedness, as opposed to the egoistic model. The new model implies a very Buddhist way of viewing things. It aligns with some Western religious beliefs as well as Eastern notions of consciousness. Of course, in the Western academic establishment there is still a lot of rejection to notions of that sort.

The way I see it, the biological, individual-centred, brain-centred model in the study of consciousness fails to recognise that we are an altricial species, i.e., that our parents, and the collective, are the ones who teach us how to function in society, provide many of the words we are going to be using the rest of our lives, socialise us, and generally guide us as to what is acceptable and what is not acceptable in social life. Schools and institutes of higher learning provide the information we require to function at the level and in the field of our choosing.

Language and culture have a huge impact on human consciousness. It is all very well to study sentience in the brain (not how it is generated there, because it is not generated by neurones or synapses), but purposely ignoring that sentience and cognition are intertwined is a huge mistake that has been costing years of effort to the scientific community.

~

Human consciousness is evidently more complex than sentience or cognition. From my perspective, it is a combination of both. This may appear obvious to some (it does to me), but it is essential to state it and emphasise it here:

- Human consciousness consists of two integrated but discrete layers:

1) basic animal consciousness, or sentience.

2) high human consciousness, or cognition.

- We are born sentient; that is a fundamental quality all mammalians inherit as part of being alive.
- Cognition is acquired through parental and collective upbringing. It is collectively and intersubjectively transmitted. In its most sophisticated form it is is only human, and its nature is cultural, i.e., it came long after sentience.
- Imagination, language, adventurousness, are exclusively human traits that follow cognition.
- Time is a human construct. It exists within cognition and only there. Past and future exist only within human cognition. Long-term memory includes identity and collective perception of that identity.

- Without cognition there is only present and change.
- Creativity and art appear to involve both an intellectual and a sentient component.

We have seen, then, that human consciousness his part existential and part cognitive.

Human consciousness is an *a priori* condition for knowledge. In the case of our species, we can acquire some knowledge through experience or habit (the hunter knows where the prey are because he's been there and seen them). But we can also think (something we acquired much later, with language).

Cognition, however, appears to have primacy over experience —it is superimposed on it and we use it much more. It is only through it that we can acquire the information we need to live in society (for instance, we can understand how a rifle operates through language and thought), and we use a lot of information in our daily lives. That has pros and cons, as we shall see.

Currently, within the study of human consciousness, Western science does not appear to contemplate the notion of a collective mind. Of course, scientists acknowledge the existence of the collective; the notions they have are clear, but science still believes the approaches to study consciousness should all be physical, begin with the individual, and be based on the brain. No interdependence is considered. No relations with other entities. At this stage, science is only focused on the way sentience emerges in the individual brain.

The fact that Western scientists want to study sentience is good. Unfortunately, their approach is wrong on two accounts. Western science hopes to reach human consciousness beginning from the study of sentience; that is impossible as, in humans, sentience has been intertwined with cognition for aeons. The task is futile. As we have stated, they have different natures, they are not a continuum. There is a ceiling between the scholar and the goal: it involves the leap from evolution to meta-evolution, that is, language and cognition. The researcher that commences the study of human consciousness from the origin of sentience will reach up to the moment of the leap into meta-evolution, but will never go beyond. Sentience and cognition have different natures, it is as simple as that.

The second point is that sentience is biological, but not really individual the way we understand individuality, because in nature there are actually no individuals or identities.

Humans have developed the notions of individuality and identity. These are secondary notions. A falcon in nature is not actually an individual, only an iteration of falcon. It may sense, or feel, as an individual, but it is part of a species and that species is part of nature.

Our ancestors did not become individuals until they slowly acquired the component of consciousness they didn't have as animals. Before then, they were only iterations of the idea of hominin. When it became necessary for them to become individuals within a group, they had to acquire an identity. Maybe things are not as simple as all that, but you get the idea, I'm sure.

Some species may have some degree of identity, especially species that are social, but that animal identity is mostly sentient: a penguin chick recognises his mother by smell. The type of identity current humans have require cognition.

Let's see how that happens: as stated, our species is altricial, that means our children require much longer than any other species to grow into adulthood. That happens because, as an animal species, humans are born sentient. But, at that stage, humans are only equipped to acquire cognition. That takes time. A toddler begins to acquire cognition when he or she learns to speak. Surely, toddlers can think well before then. But they can fully interact with other individuals only when they learn to speak. That is how language operates at any level. You can understand it before you can speak it, and you can read it before you can write it.

Adolescents become adult human beings, let's say, when they come out of the teenage years and reach their twenties.

That growth has to happen with every individual of every generation because cognition is an acquired phenomenon. The transmission of cognition necessitates that information be repeated every generation. And it is a phenomenon that continues to grow in sophistication. We learn to read and write and then we learn to use laptops, and cell phones, tablets and even smart watches.

AND NOW THAT we mention watches, let's discuss briefly the nature of time. Time is another complicated issue, but I will try to summarise this explanation as much as possible.

We know that everything changes. Change is a given. According to Aristotle, time is only the measure of change. Being a measure, time is a human creation. Animals have no time, and they have no measures or quantities either.

We need time to live in societies. The larger and more complex the society is, the more sophisticated time becomes. I repeat, time resides within cognition.

If we avoid cognition, time disappears. There is no hurry, no stress, no anxiety. All the negative connotations of time go away when you put cognition in the back burner.

Maybe we should leave this explanation for the time being. By now, though, I am sure you know what I'm getting at. That is all we need for the purposes of this book.

STUDYING an individual cannot provide an explanation for experience, as experience is beyond the individual; experience exists in a state of interconnectedness with nature. It is felt by the individual as part of a whole. The individual animal has no *subjective* experience that is separate from an *objective* reality. That is how we want to understand it in the West. The animal has sentience and, to a point, feels like an individual, but in reality, the animal just is.

As stated, individual animals are actually physical iterations of the idea of that animal (ideas are not thoughts; ideas reside within sentience; more on that later).

Predators, when they are hunting, do not stop to think "I'm looking for a particular kind of prey". The lioness, as part of her tactics and her instinct, individualises the little zebra that is running behind the herd, because that is going to be the easiest. She is aware. That's all.

In that respect, Gertrude Stein—trying to prove something else—came up with a famous sentence: *"A rose is a rose is a rose"*. There are no individual roses, just the idea of the rose. Bashō, the Japanese poet, did exactly the same thing when he described the action of a crow: *"On a withered branch/ a crow has come to perch..."*. What we have is the idea of the crow. The crow has no identity.

When we call our dog Bill, we are only anthropomorphising the dog; we give him an identity because that is the only way we have come to understand reality. We are social beings and our collective is made out of individuals. Taking that notion to extremes, Donald Duck is called Donald and his surname is Duck, and he has a sailor's outfit. Cute and funny. Human.

IN ALL PROBABILITY we are the sole witnesses of the universe. That is what we do as human beings, but especially as Western individuals; that is what our consciousness means: a subjective witnessing of the objective—separate— reality that surrounds us.

The lone jaguar, the predator, sees the prey, but he does not witness, he acts; the starling flies in a murmuration with a thousand others and maybe enjoys dawn, or sunset, but he does not ponder that dawn or that sunset. From their non-subjective perspective, they are part of the scene. They cannot extricate themselves from reality.

According to Western scholars, then, the self occurs within the thinker, and it only reaches out to where objective reality begins. We find that the self can determine what kind of thing something is, but thus far it cannot know what kind of thing *itself* is. The moment consciousness turns inwards, that knowledge should become subjective because that reality is subjective. Western scholars are trying to find out where consciousness resides in the brain. The East has already determined that it is unknowable. It is indescribable, ineffable.

More importantly, human consciousness also has a transcendental property. That means that it's irreducible to an object or a class of objects.

Neuroscience could explain where some cognitive functions occur, it could explain where some sensations occur, but it would not be able to explain consciousness as a physical entity because it not a physical entity. It is not generated by neurones either. It is exactly the other way around: neurones are generated by it. Science cannot find an answer to the existence of consciousness because the answer lies outside its bounds. Sentience may be biological, but cognition—the other component of consciousness—is not. In any case, sentience is as intersubjective as cognition.

Humans, as defined by Aristotle, are social animals. We function like birds or fish function in schools. We are not meant to operate in isolation, like certain other kinds of animals. We *need* the collective. That is how our species has developed a kind of post-biological-evolution (and this doesn't meant that biological evolution has ever stopped). Any attempt to describe a human being will find itself confronted with society as well. When we talk about human circumstances, we talk about a certain period and a certain culture. The study of human beings and their behaviour cannot be based on the individual. In any case, if that is attempted, time and place have to be included.

The essence of human consciousness—I believe—as distinct from that of other animals, is easy to discern: the functions of the brain we are born with (all of them have to do with sentience); and the ones we are equipped to acquire—cognition, intellect, or psyche—, that develop with the intervention of the collective. We are born sentient. Cognition is only acquired through parental and collective upbringing. It is culturally and individually transmitted. It is cultural by nature. We have to repeat this to ourselves if we want it to sink in. The notion is difficult to comprehend because we rarely think about it.

In order to understand how human consciousness operates, we have to imagine it within a certain society: clear evidence of it is that most psychiatric problems involve an individual that is dysfunctional, i.e., who is unable to function, or who does not function properly, within his or her social environment. If a person is physically sick, the problem is individual. It has to do with his or her individual body—although it may be contagious and, in any case, the cause of the sickness might be extraneous. Mentally ill people are people basically unfit to function within society. They may still be sentient, as that is biological, but any cognitive problem means a social problem.

Hominins only began communicating with each other in a more sophisticated manner, compared to other animals, once they grasped the meaning behind the sounds they were making. This moment, marked by the first phoneme, signifies the onset of humanity. Our evolution into humans didn't occur until one individual comprehended the message being conveyed by another individual. The origin of humanity is basically phonemic (a sound with a meaning attached to it).

Here, perhaps, we should briefly discuss artificial intelligence (AI) in order to put some ideas into context.

Attempting to find consciousness in large language models (LLMs) is going to prove impossible for several reasons, one of them is that the LLM has no sentience, its mind is not hybrid like ours. It has all the appearance of a human mind, but it cannot feel because it was not born an animal, and there is no way you can explain, or transmit the concept of sensation or feeling to a non-feeling entity. The LLM is not alive. In that respect, AI has been largely overestimated.

A text includes thoughts, ideas, feelings and sensations, but it's only the linguistic expression of those ideas, etc., thus, the LLM is a secondary iteration of the original idea, sensation or feeling, and a shallow one at that. The LLM is a human creation, a language model implanted on a machine that cannot understand how the collective (that created the language) operates. Thus far, the LLM adopts the culture of the language that is input into it without anything close to comprehension.

New ambitious projects involve more transitioning from text-centred LLMs to models with multimodal "integration". The concept sounds good, but the fact remains that AI operates within a digital environment, which does not even come close to biological (electrochemical) functions. There will never be feeling where there is no life.

SELF-AWARENESS AND IDENTITY have totally different natures. You may be self-aware when you dream, but you have no identity. Neither do you have reasoning. Normally, dreams are irrational—they make no sense. They are a product of the individual mind, but they do not include any really cognitive function. They only reproduce experience devoid of reason. We ignore their ultimate function. We are rational only when we are conscious. Cognition is used to communicate with other human beings. That is when we need to make sense. Ironically, sentience does not make sense.

I have not invented any of the words I'm using to write this, and neither has the person who reads it. We are both speakers of a language and members a culture (in my case, an adopted one).

Neuroscientists, of course, accept interaction among humans as a fact. The difference is that they assume consciousness is generated within the individual. Can that be a correct assumption? What is generated within the individual is sentience, which includes experience, it includes self-awareness, but does not include identity, for instance, which is a cognition-generated notion. Mothers—and fathers to some extent—are the ones that help generate language and cognition in the child. They only teach their babies and toddlers what, in turn, they learnt from their parents. Human cognition has necessitated transmission of information for countless generations.

Human consciousness has evolved strangely, maybe because every individual begins from scratch. Every child learns everything intersubjectively. Every child is a new hard disk drive. As Borges noticed in *The Witness,* experience is forever lost every time someone dies. One good thing is that humans have notation systems and graphemes of all sorts. Thankfully, many thoughts—and feelings—survive the individual.

This brings us to a situation on the opposite side to consciousness in AI, that is, consciousness in the newborn. AI is not a live being and will never become alive or conscious, whereas the newborn is alive but has not acquired consciousness as yet.

I imagine newborn babies have sensory experiences from birth and would venture that foetuses may even have some prenatal ones. It is possible that newbies integrate sensory and some basic cognitive experiences to respond to their new environment. Even though there are some intellectual functions that may not involve language, I would be very sceptical to the existence of any prenatal cognitive function. There seems to be cognition without language, but I would find very difficult to believe that any form of cognition could be acquired without language.

SOMEHOW,—IT seems to me—explaining human consciousness from a chronological perspective appears to provide a clearer picture: humanity originated with a 'fundamental': life, that is, our first ancestors were very basic living creatures; then they became sentient mammals; then they became one of the primate species; then language appeared among those primates—which constituted a meta-evolutionary phenomenon and added the extra layer of intellect over senses—; then human groups grew into cultures and they, in turn, grew into civilisations. In this explanation, the intellect, or cognition if you like, is acquired and transmitted through culture, and only through culture. Once information is acquired, it becomes knowledge.

Cognition, then, is subsumed within human consciousness, it becomes a human addition, a layer over our exclusively-animal-consciousness, but the analysis—I believe—is clearer by means of the chronological explanation. To borrow from (microcosmic) existentialist terminology, *existence* precedes *essence*. I would add, *we are* [biologically animal] before *we become* [culturally human]. What is interesting in all of this is that, chronologically, it applies to the individual as well as the collective. There is also a circularity to it: a human individual initiated culture; and culture keeps on creating human individuals, if you like.

LANGUAGE AND CULTURE

"A great stride in the development of the intellect will have followed, as soon as the half-art and half-instinct of language came into use; for the continued use of language will have reacted on the brain and produced an inherited effect; and this again will have reacted on the improvement of language. As Mr. Chauncey Wright has well remarked, the largeness of the brain in man relatively to his body, compared with the lower animals, may be attributed in chief part to the early use of some simple form of language,- that wonderful engine which affixes signs to all sorts of objects and qualities, and excites trains of thought which would never arise from the mere impression of the senses, or if they did arise could not be followed out. The higher intellectual powers of man, such as those of ratiocination, abstraction, self-consciousness, &c., probably follow from the continued improvement and exercise of the other mental

faculties..".-

Charles Darwin, *Descent of Man*

---

*I*n *Descent of Man* it is possible to appreciate that Darwin himself could see the effect that language (and culture, of course) had had on the human brain. He could see the feedback-loop that had acted on the adaptive brain and produced the growth of the neocortex. Darwin guessed that— at a certain point in time—there had been a massive leap (meta-evolutionary, I would add) that placed *H. sapiens* well beyond sentience and any other species.

It is not that human intellect is entirely dependent upon language, but it could be said that there is a pre-linguistic human consciousness and a linguistic one. Their natures are totally different: one appeared with life as a natural phenomenon, whereas the other one emerged as the inter-subjective explosion of information and knowledge that continues growing to this day.

As already stated, our minds operate at two different levels in order to achieve two different ends.

One layer of the mind—sentience—is there to keep our individual bodies alive. Like all other mammalians, we need our senses to see, smell, hear, taste and touch. They allow us to move unimpeded in our surroundings, enjoy food or music; see, smell or hear predators, enemies, or sexual partners; and recognise familiar shapes and textures with our fingers or toes when we cannot see them, among other life activities we require to survive as individuals. That layer is totally related to biology, totally physical. It is a result of evolution and all mammalians have it.

The biological part of our consciousness, which is also the 'emotional' one, concentrates mostly on survival, it regulates body temperature, breathing and heartbeat, for instance. That is the animal (as opposed to human) component. Whenever there is trauma, or danger, the mind initiates its response: flight or fight. All kinds of chemicals flood our body, from adrenaline to cortisol. Rational thought is absent. The subconscious is also at play, the way it happens in dreams.

That component is the one that allowed our ancestors (and still allows other animals) to function as integral parts of the wholeness.

At the beginning of this chapter, we saw that Charles Darwin had guessed that language greatly influenced cognition. He could surmise that dualism provided a good explanation for consciousness. The nineteenth century was a period when the only option he had was to choose between materialism or religion. He chose materialism. He often repeated that human beings were too proud to believe in anything but Creation: *"Man in his arrogance thinks himself a great work, worthy the interposition of a deity, more humble & I believe true to consider him created from animals"*.

Language and cognition appear to develop almost simultaneously. In fact, we don't know whether there is actual human intellect without any language. Indeed, it would be very difficult to imagine humanity without language.

Some written languages are so finely tuned that they allow thought be transmitted directly, although they usually have some phonetic component. Chinese and Japanese ideograms — *kanji* in Japanese, *hanzi* in Chinese—may convey ideas without the use of sound. The idea can be visually processed directly by the brain. For instance, 竹 means "bamboo" in both, Chinese and Japanese. In Japanese it's pronounced [taːke]; in Chinese it is [tzūdzə] with slight tone variations from Cantonese to Mandarin. The symbol is the same. These graphemes, these ideograms, are actually units of meaning. They don't represent individual sounds, that is, the reader reads the same symbol in his or her own language.

Of course, humans can think without producing any vocal sounds. That is called "inner speech". Some toddlers tend to vocalise their thoughts for a while, until they discover they don't need to do it. Most humans have that inner voice, which helps them articulate thought more clearly in their mind. The strength of that articulation is such, that often—especially while reading—the larynx produces minuscule reflex movements that accompany the inner voice.

If we think literacy commenced millennia ago, reading without making any sound is a fairly recent innovation. At a time when people would only read aloud, St Augustine marvelled at St Ambrose reading in silence:

"But when he read, his eyes glided through the pages and his heart searched for meaning, but his voice and tongue rested. Often, when we went to see him (because no one was forbidden to enter, nor did he want anyone to be announced to come to see him), we would see him like this, reading to himself...". Someone, in silence, acquires information from symbols. Quite

remarkable. Augustine cannot stop wondering about his own consciousness.

"How come I have consciousness"—Augustine says—*"and animals don't?" "I turn to myself and ask myself, 'Who are you?' and 'One Man' will answer. And I find that in me there is a soul, and a body; one outside, and the other, inside me. ... Animals, large and small, can see the body, but they cannot be asked, because they have no use of reason besides their senses to judge what they see. Men can do it..."* What's interesting is that Augustine sees that he is partly his body, and that his soul is *"inside"* that body. In other words, he places his self-awareness in an intermediate place between body and soul. But then Augustine lives in a period when psyche is not consciousness but a soul given to us by God.

In this chapter we are discussing language and culture. Apart from gesturing—which often implies language, or is included in language—what is involved in communication between human individuals is a mutually intelligible language. That means that, to communicate with a certain degree of sophistication, individuals need to belong to the same culture and use the same language.

IF TIME IS A HUMAN CONSTRUCT—AS I, among others, claim—that developed within human culture, or a device that we use to explain our long-term episodic memory, time exists only within human culture. Depending on their need, it is possible for some cultures not to have developed the concept of time altogether, or to have developed a partial, or different, concept of time from what we consider "normal" in the West.

Recently, a study conducted at Osaka University discovered that daydreaming produced special patterns in brain activity. The study confirms what Gautama realised many centuries ago. Change and suffering and death are only the result of human thought beyond the present. These self-generated thoughts result in special ripples in the hippocampus—in which memories are formed and from which they are retrieved. Mind-wandering, which only happens in humans, is the result of imagined future scenarios, reminiscences about the past (e.g. guilt and regret for things we did or omitted to do), and hypothetical fears. There is no doubt, time—a product of human cognition—is the main origin of stress and unhappiness.

We experience and interpret reality the way we do because we are predisposed by our language and by the way our culture perceives it.

THE PIRAHÃ, a fairly isolated Amazonian tribe, are probably a good example of linguistic relativity, i.e., that thought is affected by language and vice versa, in a feedback loop. The Pirahã language—which is from the Amazon—like some Melanesian ones, lacks cardinal numbers after "one" and "two", even though Pirahã speakers understand larger quantities; it has no colours except "light" and "dark" (it has other ways of explaining colours: "like-blood", for red); and it includes a system of pronouns—that can also become nouns—that, for Westerners, is extremely difficult to understand.

To give you an idea of the difficulty involved in understanding Pirahã grammar, their verbal system has a quantity of aspects: perfective (completed), imperfective (incomplete), telic (reaching a goal), atelic, repeated, and commencing; but they have very little transitivity. It appears fairly clear that the way the Pirahã language has developed is a reflection of the way they perceive the world. Languages and cultures develop according to the needs of a particular group of speakers in a given environment.

Another culture that disproves the complete universality of language are the Amondawa, also another fairly uncontacted Amazonian tribe. They do not have a word for "time". When asked to find an equivalent to the Portuguese word for time, *"tempo"*, they came up with their word for "sun". They don't appear to conceive of time as a flowing, measurable, framework for change. These examples may eventually prove that the notion of time is shaped by culture. Coincidentally, speakers of Kuuk Thayorre, in Queensland, Australia, when faced with some temporal progressions (e.g., same man, different ages), tend to follow, in their thinking, the trajectory of the sun.

HUMANS CAN IMAGINE things that do not exist, and they can do it individually or collectively. Yuval Noah Harari adds that human language has an extraordinary quality that is lacking in any other form of animal communication: apart from imagining non-existent things individually, humans can share those ideas and express them collectively.

Humans can add an extra layer to reality: they can create a special social reality and invent the rules that apply to that collective. They are the constitutive rules that are understood and respected by all members of that society. From the time we are toddlers, humans are taught increasingly complex systems of rules that we will need to abide by in order to live within society. Those complex, intangible concepts are transmitted only because human language is capable of expressing and sharing them.

George Steiner elegantly explains the complex nature of the phenomenon:

"Language is assuredly material in that it requires the play of muscle and vocal cords; but it is also impalpable and, by virtue of inscription and remembrance, free of time, though moving in temporal flow".

So, the way things are, neuroscientists are looking for the correlates where sentience and cognition are generated by neurones. They want to find out where sentience and cognition become experience. How do we know that we feel something? How do we know that we know something? Their search leads nowhere because the question they formulate is the wrong one. Neurones are created by experience, not the other way around, and sentience is biological, whereas cognition is cultural, just as language is cultural.

Sentience and cognition have developed in such a way that they are distinct but integrated layers. The layers cannot be peeled away rationally. Only meditation can do it.

A very comprehensive study conducted by Andalusian and American researchers discovered that there was *"... a network of 4,000 genes that clustered into multiple modules that were expressed in specific regions of the brain. Some of these genes had already been linked in previous studies to the inheritance of human personality"*. The genes were subdivided into two sub-networks: *"One network regulated emotional reactivity (anxiety, fear, etc.), while the other regulated what a person perceives as meaningful (e.g., production of concepts and language)."*.

The findings appear to support the ideas behind this book: 'two discrete but intertwined layers (*"networks of genes expressed in the brain"*) of human consciousness': a sentient, biological one (*"anxiety, fear, etc."*) and a cognitive, meta-evolutionary one (*"e.g., production of concepts and language"*).

Linguists know that only in rare instances there is real, direct, correspondence between two or more languages. Translators and interpreters, of course, are even more aware of that because they experience it in their day-to-day work. Those differences appear at all grammatical levels.

Of course, it is possible to look for a universal origin of language or state that we are born with, a *"tabula rasa"* template in our brains that allows us to input and use any language. Nobody denies that we can learn any language. Of course, we can understand other cultures. The shared humanity of all races is a fact with which linguistic relativity is not concerned.

But also, what is impossible to deny is that culture and language form a tight feedback loop. The translation of a concept may involve a philosophical worldview that does not occur in the target language. In those cases, the expressions are really untranslatable. At least, when they are translated, they do not include every nuance that the interlocutor is meant to receive.

A good example would be どぞよろしく (dozou yoroshiku), in Japanese. In general, that means "pleased to meet you", so it can be translated with those exact words, but the actual meaning is "please take care of me" or "please, treat me favourably". A more formal way to say it in Japanese would be どぞよろしくおねがいします (dozou yoroshiku onegai shimasu), which can be translated as "how do you do?". But it actually means "I am so grateful for any support you may provide to me" or words to that effect. "Please" is included twice in the sentence, in different forms. English speakers find the concepts hard to understand. "How do you do?" sounds much better. That is how translation works, or appears to work. When that happens, the translator or interpreter knows that the semantic cultural transfer has not actually occurred, i.e., the actual meaning, the high degree of respect to the other person implied, has not come through (and cannot come through, or be understood, when the interlocutor is monolingual).

A Western mind finds that level of respect almost impossible to understand. The other side of the coin is that an Asian mind finds the Western individual extremely solipsistic, to the point of being often culturally unacceptable. To the Asian ear, Westerners often sound rude. There are historical, philosophical and religious reasons for both sides to think that way, and that is part of the story we're telling in this book.

The example I have just provided is an extreme one. There are countless examples like that one, though.

Studies of cultural/linguistic conditioning that confirm Linguistic Relativity are beginning to be conducted more often, as researchers commence to accept the possibility of a non-universalist framework for the study of consciousness. Any monolingual person, on encountering a different culture —when they find themselves among people who speak a different language— often experience what is known as "culture shock". The characteristics of their language involve another perspective of the world. Humboldt used to say that different languages reflect different worldviews, that language forms thought. And, indeed, there is a loop: words shape thoughts and vice versa.

WHEN DID we acquire human culture? Let's see what Rebecca Wragg-Sykes' (*Kindred - Neanderthal Love, Life, Death and Art*) comparisons with our *Neanderthal* ancestors tell us about *H. sapiens* culture. She wonders: *"Could there really have been a 'light-bulb moment' when some novel genetic mutation or combination greatly increased H. sapiens tendencies towards more formalised artistic traditions, or flashy burials? Again, the reality is inconveniently uncertain."*.

Her assumption about *"some novel genetic mutation"* appears to be close to what neuroscientists believe. The reality may be uncertain, but common sense seems to dictate that *H. sapiens* were further advanced in the long process of the acquisition of language. When compared to *Neanderthals*, *H. sapiens*, who lived in larger groups, appears to have had a more developed (maybe recursive?) language that allowed for a more elaborate artistic expression and treatment of the dead.

Humboldt thought that literature led to the essence of a language. This, he believed, was the "spirit of the language". Linguistics, however, developed basically by studying language in terms of form rather than depth, rather than essence. In a way, Humboldt's ideas were more concerned with the way some aspects of a culture coincide with the development of its language and vice versa.

During the twentieth century, linguists generally believed that their discipline had to be considered as a serious (hard?) science, rather than something closer to the humanities. The way language may influence cognition and the way culture may influence language were taken as foggy areas that were outside their field.

INTEREST IN EASTERN MYSTICISM

"I don't wanta hear all your word descriptions of words words words you made up all winter, man I wanta be enlightened by actions."

Jack Kerouac - *The Dharma Bums*

"I went to the woods because I wished to live deliberately, to front only the essential facts of life, and see if I could not learn what it had to teach."

Henry David Thoreau - *Walden*

"Just as the farmer irrigates a field, a fletcher fashions an arrow, and a carpenter shapes a piece of wood, so the sage tames his self."

Gautama Buddha - *Dhammapada*

The first contacts with the East, those of travellers like Marco Polo, for instance, were few and far between. Europe was extremely interested in commerce with the East but also in their art, religions and philosophies. However, there was a physical obstacle between Europe and the far East: Islam.

Here, perhaps we should include some historical context. From the beginning of the eighth century, the Iberian Peninsula was invaded and occupied by the Moors. Europe was surrounded by warlike Muslim nations who made access to trade and contact with the Far East extremely difficult. Barbary Coast pirates and Ottomans roamed the Mediterranean, terrorising European coastal populations. The Crusades attempted to break through, but eventually failed. In 1453, as explained, Constantinople fell to the Ottoman Turk. The city was the last bastion left of what had been the main Christian Empire: Byzantium. By 1492, after the fall of the Muslim Kingdom of Granada to the Catholic Monarchs, Europe—especially the Iberian Peninsula—started its expansion to gain access to trade, particularly to spices, which were vital to keep foodstuffs edible for longer periods. The Portuguese and the Spanish commenced their expeditions towards what they called "the Indies" around Africa and across the Atlantic respectively. The Ottomans kept on advancing deep into Europe until 1571, when the Holy League—a coalition of Catholic states—inflicted a massive naval defeat on them at Lepanto. The Mediterranean was back in European hands. In the meantime, Portuguese and Spanish caravels had reached India, China and Japan. That was the beginning of a European fascination with their culture, philosophies and religions.

By the seventeenth and eighteenth centuries, Europeans had adopted decorative styles called *'chinoiserie'*, which copied Chinese motifs and techniques in furniture and textiles.

But in Japan, after Portuguese Jesuit missionaries achieved their first conversions to Christianity in the 16th century, the Tokugawa Shogunate, afraid of Western influence, closed the country for more than two hundred years (to understand this period, I recommend *'Silence'*, a movie by Martin Scorsese).

In 1852-54, the American Navy, under Admiral Perry, imposed the opening of trade which resulted in the Meiji Restoration. The West, again, became fascinated by the East and its aesthetics. *'Japanned'* lacquer work imitated the sophisticated work of Japanese craftsmen, and Giacomo Puccini composed *'Madama Butterfly'*.

The reopening of contact meant that people like Ernest Fenollosa, an American academic, could devote his life to the study of Japanese art, culture and literature. Fenollosa lived some time in Japan and eventually converted to Buddhism. He, and his assistant, Okakura Kakuzō, were highly influential in a revival of Japanese culture and a renewed academic interest in Buddhism in the West.

During the time of his studies, Fenollosa discovered some ancient Chinese scrolls. Travelling monks had taken those rolls with the teachings of Buddha from China to Japan. Many of his discoveries were important. On Fenollosa's death, his widow donated his writings to Ezra Pound, who published translations of Chinese poetry and Noh theatre plays. In the meantime, authors like Herman Hesse (*Siddharta, The Glass Bead Game*) and sometime later Alan W Watts ('*The way of Zen*', '*The Book*') introduced principles and practices to Western readers, or hinted about them in stories and novels.

During the nineteen fifties and sixties, Beat Generation writers Jack Kerouac (*On the Road, The Dharma Bums*) and Allen Ginsberg, among others, began exploring Eastern ways and customs and experimenting with drugs. The American counterculture in particular based itself, in those days, on Eastern philosophy and mysticism. Some authors, thinkers and artists understood the profound differences that existed between their culture and the East, and were eager to explore them. Others—shallower in their approach—were only curious because of the 'mysterious and exotic' nature of the East.

With his book '*An introduction to Zen Buddhism*', D.T. Suzuki, a Japanese academic and translator, who taught in several Western and Japanese universities, did a lot to popularise Eastern culture in the West.

From experimentations with meditation and Eastern art, literary vanguard artists, encouraged by academics like

Timothy Leary, went directly to mushrooms, LSD, peyote and other psychedelic drugs. An offshoot of that was Carlos Castañeda's '*The teachings of Don Juan*', followed by a series of books on shamanism that were mainly fictional.

Of course, since the twenties and thirties there had been isolated Western thinkers and philosophers who had dabbled in Eastern concepts of consciousness. Michel Foucault, for instance, and his attention to relationships; Wittgenstein, who famously stated something very close to Zen: *"Whereof one cannot speak, thereof one must be silent"*; and eminently, Schrödinger, the physicist famous for his cat in a box paradox. He established a very clear relationship between Buddhism and quantum physics at a time when those comparisons were not taken seriously. Schrödinger however had the stature to be able to do it (and a Nobel Prize that backed him up).

JORGE LUIS BORGES gave several lectures on Buddhism and, in the late seventies, wrote a book with Alicia Jurado titled *What is Buddhism?* Although fascinated by it since childhood, Borges himself admitted he had never understood it. That becomes evident from the book, and from his essays and lectures on the life of Gautama Buddha; for instance: *"Reality may be too complex for oral transmission; legends recreate it in a way that is only accidentally false and which permits it to travel through the world, from mouth to mouth"* (from *Forms of a Legend, Other Inquisitions*). As an explanation of Buddhist rejection of cognition, it fails twice: what cannot be transmitted orally is the sentient perception of reality; also, *'legend'* (which etymologically comes from Latin *'legere'*, 'to read'), is even less acceptable to transmit the essence of Buddhism.

Borges discusses Buddhism like a religion, which may be partially true in certain areas, but that does not explain any of the essence of Buddhism. Several times he talks about *'faith'*; again, he does it from the perspective of religious, or Christian, faith, from a very Western perspective.

The irony is that Borges, for all his universal brilliance and erudition, remained essentially an Argentine (with a strong European background), and could only perceive the East as an outsider.

And what's even more interesting is that, stories like *The Writing of the God* or *The Circular Ruins* are eminently Buddhist stories.

One thing that blew my mind was the similarity between the essence of *The Aleph* and one of Dōgen's expressions on the experience of *satori*: *"The entire world can be found in the most minute of particles"*.

THE HIPPIE MOVEMENT took over from the Beatniks. George Harrison, later followed by the rest of *The Beatles*, befriended several Asian musicians—Ravi Shankar being the main star among them—which gave an incredible boost to the incursion into Eastern culture.

Following the musical and philosophical trend established by celebrities, many young people travelled to the East, especially India and Japan, looking for alternative ways and enlightenment in schools, *ashrams* and Zen monasteries. There were real *gurus, saddhus* and *swamis*, and bogus ones. Jiddu Krishnamurti was a real philosopher and author who wrote several books and had a huge following in the West. Others, like Bhagwan Shree Rajneesh (aka Osho), created cults that gathered thousands of adepts, with promises of alternative enlightenment that proved baseless. Bhagwan founded *Rajneeshpuran*, a massive *ashram* in Oregon, in the 1980s but was eventually deported from the United States under suspicions of criminal activities.

A young Steve Jobs, like so many of his generation, did his pilgrimage to India to find enlightenment. His devotion to Eastern thought and Zen Buddhism continued throughout his life. As the polymath and a business genius who found the connection between technology, design and the humanities, he probably gained some pleasure, maybe happiness, and shared some of that happiness among Apple devotees. But—I would venture—as an autistic man, enlightenment escaped him. According to Walter Isaacson, his biographer, he remained a Westerner at heart.

Apart from the contacts between East and West, the differences in their approaches to consciousness have kept both cultures as separate entities with few points in common.

Surprisingly, quantum mechanics has now (long after Schrödinger was ridiculed for it) reached a point where there is a kind of agreement with Buddhism. In the seventies, a book by Frijof Capra, a physicist (*'The Tao of Physics'*) discussed exactly that.

INTEREST IN EASTERN MYSTICISM

Nowadays, more and more scientists agree that quantum mechanics does not seem to work together well with the concept of an objective reality (on which—let me repeat—Western philosophy and science are based). One interpretation of quantum mechanics, however, appears to mesh seamlessly with Buddhist 'philosophy'.

In the West there is, then, a renewed acceptance of the principles of Buddhism. Buddhism, in any case, doesn't need to prove a thing. It just is.

BUDDHISM IN INDIA AND CHINA

"Of course you are uncertain, Kalamas. Of course you are in doubt. When there are reasons for doubt, uncertainty is born. So in this case, Kalamas, don't go by reports, by legends, by traditions, by scripture, by logical conjecture, by inference, by analogies, by agreement through pondering views, by probability, or by the thought, 'This contemplative is our teacher.' When you know for yourselves that, 'These qualities are bad; these qualities are blameworthy; these qualities are censured by the wise; these qualities, when adopted & carried out, lead to harm & to suffering' — then you should abandon them."

Gautama Buddha - *Kalama Sutta*

> *"Buddhist philosophers, over centuries of discussion with their Indian philosophical interlocutors, have given compelling reasons to reject the intelligibility and existence of intrinsic properties. Their arguments have inspired analytical philosophers and quantum physicists to maintain the primacy of relations over entities with intrinsic properties."*
>
> Frank, Gleiser & Thompson - *The Blind Spot*

The fact that Buddhism appeared in India when there were already large cities in the subcontinent should come as no surprise. For a long time, human beings lived in small clans. Up to that point, human instincts had adapted without much problem to living in groups larger than clans but smaller than cities; tribes appear to have been a —still comfortable—limit for the individual. Before then, the hunter-gatherer setting was a situation in which humans functioned very well. Civilisation complicated matters a lot.

Like any other social animals, humans, when placed in crowded situations, suffer all kinds of issues, like competitive stress derived from a lower social status or rank, depressive moods, anxiety, or even an inefficient immune system. The desire for prestige or fame, wealth and material possessions occurs only in large civilisations. In smaller groups, it is non-existent.

It is quite possible that the transition between living in hunter-gatherer groups, —even agricultural groups— and life in a city may have been quite traumatic for some. Apparently, cities in India had the equivalent of gated communities, where the more affluent groups enjoyed their privileges, to the exclusion of the majority, which had to labour without much freedom.

The appearance of fakirs, yogis and other mendicants around the first Indian cities could not have been a coincidence. These were people who could not integrate, and people who found that the competition they had to suffer in order to possess material things within the city was not worth the effort. Life was suffering. There was kind of a nostalgia for a simpler type of life.

A mixture between hippiedom and socialism, Buddhism surged from Hinduism as a rejection to the brutality of civilisation. Here, the comparison with Christianity is also very interesting.

Gautama combined the feelings of many of those—voluntary or involuntary—outcasts. He agglutinated their emotions and provided the motives they needed for their choice. What he preached was a reactive kind of non-attachment (to things or people). A return to the more basic existence they craved, but with a motivation. Civilisation required a lot of thought (and a life in which sentience was dimmed); human beings could find a much more enjoyable life through basic experience and without material possessions. Nothing lasts forever, things change. Why attach ourselves to things that will not last? At what price? But the most important thing he preached was acceptance to whatever happens in the present. Acceptance was wisdom.

Wisdom was the closest to happiness humans could hope for. Contentment.

We know that Buddhism in India—like Christianity in Judea—began, literally, in the periphery of the main religion, in this case, Hinduism.

While Christianity rejected sacrifice, revenge, and violence in general—and we can see that in Matthew's spurning of Talion Law and in Christ's advice to turn the other cheek, among other things— it generally accepted the growth of society and civilisation in Judea, and asked people to join the sect.

Western monastic orders were part of a larger institution—the Church—and operated within its framework. Mystics and hermits were not a generalised phenomenon, nor were they as noticeable as they were in the East.

Although he lived in a cave in the desert, John the Baptist, Jesus' relative and mentor, invited people into the larger community and, in accepting them, gave them a communal identity. He baptised crowds in the Jordan river.

Gautama Buddha, on the other hand, became a hermit himself and rejected larger societies altogether. What is clear from his teachings is that he did not believe that thought, logic, conjecture, inference, or analogy could lead anywhere near peace and acceptance of reality. Nothing but direct experience provided a valid answer to the needs of the individual. The communion he was looking for was with nature rather than with society. He rejected anything he considered vaguely artificial.

It is easy to conclude that Gautama had guessed the dual nature of human consciousness which, in larger societies, was reaffirmed by the introduction of extensive use of thought, language, and writing. His rejection of anything related to the intellect and his quest for peace on the basis of a return to direct sentience appears to confirm this. But his greatest discovery was the inner being and its oneness with nature. Sentience, he discovered, was the way to *nirvana*. Utter wisdom comes only from direct experience.

Of course, the different philosophies adopted by Gautama and Jesus produced very different results. The West ended up with a highly individualistic society whereas, in the East, the individual accepts the rules of the group to a much larger extent. Intersubjectiveness is of paramount importance in Eastern societies.

The paradox is that Christianity insists on a 'communion of sorts'… society is always placed above the individual, whereas Buddhism strongly advises and looks for an inner 'spiritual' experience seemingly centred on the individual.

IN THIS CHAPTER, I quote Gautama, when he tells the Kalamas that, if they doubt, they should abandon any practices that are not what they had expected. The Kalamas had been visited by Brahmins, who said that their truth—Brahmin truth—was the only real one.

Gautama told the Kalamas that, if they doubted, if they thought what the Brahmins had told them was not true, if they thought it could lead to suffering, they should abandon that belief. He told them to go and find out for themselves. Gautama also advised them against *"scripture, ... logical conclusions... or ... thought"*. By that he meant, *"do not accept explanations, only experience"*...

Buddhist scripture sees Gautama as someone who really emerges from Hinduism with a different search altogether. He is like the Martin Luther of the East. The revelation comes directly from the gods. At one point, in the old Pali texts, Brahma descends from the heavens with a large retinue and asks Gautama to commence preaching, as his preaching would save mankind. Gautama agrees.

But Gautama—we find out later—is not looking for God. That requires imagining that there is a God or gods. Gautama preaches focusing on something that is as far away from the divinity as possible: he suggests looking at oneself and searching for the inner being. The world—he says—is contingent. Change is inevitable, as is suffering. There is inevitability in being born, growing up, getting sick, growing old and dying. All of that has to do with time. None of that has anything to do with the present.

After agreeing with Brahma's request, he goes to Vanarasi, begs for alms and looks for five monks who were ascetic friends of his. He shows them the Middle Path, which lies between carnal life and ascetic life. The monks convert to Buddhism.

In the Middle Path, which he preaches, Gautama says there are four truths: suffering, the cause of suffering, the end of suffering, and the path that leads to the end of suffering.

One interesting principle that emerges from the Middle Path is that it rejects asceticism—in which the individual uses prayer or mortification, and the body is made to suffer to achieve a higher end— and it also rejects carnal desires, which eventually result in suffering. What is left is a natural life of acceptance with no indulgence but no denial either. The Middle Path looks for a sophisticated kind of reunion with nature: the discovery of the inner being.

THERE MUST HAVE BEEN a real Buddha as well as the mythical one. In India chronology was not important at the time (they still appear not to be that keen on lists of kings and battles). So, all we have left is the mythical Buddha. In any case, it would be a waste to try to narrate what the legend says about him. For instance, telling a Western audience that the Buddha entered his mother from one of her sides in the shape of a young white elephant with six tusks would not mean anything to them.

We know some details that appear to be real, like the fact that Siddharta Gautama was twenty-nine years old when he commenced preaching. We also know that, before that, he had several teachers. Contrary to what legend says, his father appears to have been a rich Nepalese landowner from Kapilavastu, not a king.

What precedes Buddhism is a Hindu philosophy called *Samkhya*. Basically, *Samkhya* is a dualist conception of human reality: there is *Purusha*, a male witness-consciousness, which cannot be defined or analysed, and *Prakriti*, a female consciousness, which includes cognitive, moral, psychological, emotional, sensorial and physical aspects of reality. Between *Purusha* and *Prakriti* lies *Buddhi*. Is that the origin of the Middle Path?

In *Samkhya* we can see a germ of Buddhism. But there are also big differences. *Samkhya* delights in analysing and enumerating (I am trying not to include any of the lists in Pali or Sanskrit here as they only cause confusion).

Purusha sounds a bit like *nirvana* or *satori*. Also, there appears to be a linguistic connection that is interesting to note: *Prakriti*, the word, has a strong similarity to the *Prakrits*, the languages that descend from Sanskrit. So, for *Samkhya*, language (mostly intellect?) and real wisdom seem to be on opposite sides of reality.

Also preceding actual Buddhism is *Vedānta*, a philosophy of wisdom and salvation that for millennia was transmitted orally. It is a kind of pantheistic monism. Only the present is important.

The *Vedānta* claims that man continues living exactly the same after *nirvana*, like the potter's wheel keeps on spinning after the pot is finished. One famous Zen saying is "*Before satori, chopping wood and carrying water; after satori, chopping wood and carrying water*". Enlightenment does not change the enlightened. In many ways, it's imperceptible.

But there is no need to dwell much longer on these ancient practices. For our purposes, the Indian religions, philosophies and disciplines that preceded Buddhism only complicate matters.

Even the followers of Buddha made things more difficult by adding rites, enumerations, roles, explanations and superstitions. What interests us is how Zen emerged from all these convoluted theories. How Zen acquired the elegant simplicity it has.

The essence was there: Buddha himself rejected abstract debates and came up with the famous parable of the man who, wounded by an arrow, does not want to have it removed until he knows the name, caste, nationality and other details of the archer who fired the shot. Buddha said that doing that was running the risk of death. "I am here to teach how to remove the arrow" he said. According to him, all other speculations were useless.

Buddha claimed that the highest state a human can aim at is ecstasy, which is achieved by means of meditative concentration. *Nirvana* is the only form of salvation. Buddhism, from the beginning, rejects the separate existences of consciousness and matter, subject and object, soul and deity (one reality). There is only a dream that has no dreamer. The dream is surrounded by nothingness.

Gautama made a clear distinction between relying on, or attaching ourselves to, something or someone outside of our true self. It may bring temporary pleasure but that is all. He preached non-attachment. Pleasure vanishes because it is artificial; paradoxically, it is based on separation. It comes from the outside in. Joy flows from the inside out. Attachment brings transient pleasure, which will eventually disappear and bring pain. Non-attachment means lasting joy.

Identities need to be satisfied, they need external possessions, that is, things and people (!) and riches. But there are other possessions that are intangible, like social status and physical appearance, fame and recognition. In any case, once the individual needs possessions, the need will never disappear, that individual will need more and more. When you take those away—and that is bound to happen because possessions and relationships are transient—the individual suffers.

Gautama never intended to found a religion. His sole aim was teaching how to free his disciples from the world of appearances. *Nirvana* breaks the cycle of reincarnations. That is the end of suffering.

Advaida Vedānta is considered as a school which is still part of Hinduism. The difference with *Theravāda* Buddhism is that *Vedānta* claims there is no difference between subject and object (the unity of *Atman* and *Brahman*), whereas *Theravāda* goes one step further and claims the non duality of reality. Buddha rejected the *Vedas* (or texts). However, his teachings resulted in texts like the *Pali* Canon, or *Tripitaka* (three *Pitakas* or chapters), which is a massive (sixty-odd volumes) collection of teachings and doctrine.

Hinayana doctrine (the Little Vehicle) is the first version of Buddhism proper, *Mahayana* (the Great Vehicle) makes its appearance around the second century CE. *Mahayana*, pretty much like *Samkhya,* is full of divisions and subdivisions, enumerations, negations and affirmations. Both doctrines share the notions of impermanence of the self, suffering and the unreality of the ego. They also share the Four Noble Truths, Karma and the Middle Path. Both doctrines reject causality. Things just happen. The individual does not exist in isolation.

In Tibet, *Mahayana* becomes Lamaism, which is institutionalised as a theocracy, where there are many rites and hierarchies. The Dalai Lama is the head of state and the

Pantchen Lama is the head of government. The current Dalai Lama lives in exile in India, after the occupation of Tibet by communist China in 1949.

How Buddhism travelled eastwards, towards China, becomes an interesting step in the history of the philosophy or practice, which in certain places becomes a religion. What happens in China is fairly complicated. The approximate date when that happened is not quite certain. In any case Buddhism had to face a centuries-old tradition of Confucianism. Taoism was another important force founded, like Confucianism, in the sixth century BCE.

What is certain is that Buddhism became really influential around the sixth century of our era. Bodhidharma arrived in China in 526 CE. There are many stories about the patriarch in China. According to legend, he spent nine years meditating before a wall, where his image became imprinted; he later founded *Ch'an,* the meditation sect. Meditation involved sitting cross-legged, in what is called the "lotus position", what became *zazen* in Japanese, and engaging in concentration using several different methods, like repeating a *koan* or a mantra, or silently reciting the name of a Buddha.

Ch'an simplified things. There was a total rejection of the convoluted explanations and the sixty-odd volumes of the Pali Canon or any other ancient texts. The path could not be explained with words. Even the statues of Buddha were not there to be worshipped. *Ch'an* meant that the person had to experience enlightenment directly. There was no substitute for experience because it was all that was.

Ch'an, as we know, went to Japan, where it became Zen.

So, there being no more words, no more Pali Canon, no more deities to be worshipped, what was the result of that transformation? You cannot call Zen a religion, as there is no worship involved. You cannot call Zen a philosophy either, because there is no rational quest to explain anything. Buddhism grew out of a philosophy that rejected Hinduism, a polytheistic religion—and it actually became a religion itself, again, in Tibet. Then it crossed into China, where it became a way of life.

Zen is, in many ways, an oxymoron. Far from being a religion, its practitioners are mendicant (but working) monks of some sort, if that makes any sense. It absolutely rejects thought, or any form of logic or intellectual activity. Without allowing questions, it provides the most transcendental answer to any human individual: how to enjoy life and find a meaning for it. Further than that, although it is a type of mysticism, it establishes that you should not reject your body, on the contrary, it tells you that you should look for your inner body.

To a mind used to Christian mystics, individuals like St Catherine of Siena, St Francis of Assisi, St Rose of Lima, or St Ignatius of Loyola, people who aspired to a spiritual union with God and rejected their flesh as the core of sin, the emphasis on physicality that Zen advocates is difficult to understand. Looking for the union between your body and nature—reality and being—doesn't quite seem like mysticism. The difference, perhaps, lies in the fact that Zen does not recognise a spiritual or supernatural reality. What replaces mortification in Zen is discipline and method. Both, together, eventually produce a strong but different type of moral character in the follower.

Christian mystics wish to achieve a trance and that trance takes them to a special union with God, and that follows a certain logic. There is a method: denial of the flesh leads to a spiritual existence. In the East, the approach is a much more wholistic one. There are no differences or definitions of the good or bad sides of humanity. Zen advocates the comprehensive understanding of the whole. There is a synthesis. At a special point, the follower reaches the union it looks for, but not with God. The union is with mother nature.

To the outsider, Zen appears to be some kind of occult practice. The results, however, are there. And there is no magic involved, it's only that the methods are not as defined and clear as the Western mind would want them to be. Nothing is obvious. The methods and principles are totally intuitive; they are vague and ill-defined to say the least (far from clear, until the student grasps how the change happens in the form of an epiphany).

In actual fact, Zen is a highly refined kind of practical mysticism. It is the essence of Buddhism—what became of Buddhism after centuries of searching, until it reached Japan.

JAPAN AND ZEN

"How hard, then, and yet how easy it is to understand the truth of Zen! Hard because to understand it is not to understand it; easy because not to understand it is to understand it. A Master declares that even Buddha Sakyamuni and Bodhisatva Maitreya do not understand it, where simple-minded knaves do understand it."

D.T. Suzuki - *An Introduction to Zen Buddhism*

我と来て遊べや親のない雀
— 小林一茶
"Wareto kite asobe ya oya no nai suzume"
"Come play with me, little orphan sparrow."
Kobayashi Issa

遠山や目玉に写るとんぼかな
— 小林一茶

"Tōyama ya medama ni utsuru tonbo ka na"
"Distant mountains
Reflected in the eyes
Of a dragonfly"
— *Kobayashi Issa*

Mahayana Buddhism made its first entrance into Japan in the sixth-century, but it was not a grand entrance; it was a strange one, and one that says tons about the nature of the doctrine.

The rulers of the Yamato Court, in Nara, had taken over all agricultural land in Japan and had managed to suppress the main clans. Their government was strong.

In 538 CE, the King of Baekje, one the small kingdoms of Korea, needed assistance from the powerful Yamato Court. With his delegation, the Korean King sent a golden image of Buddha, together with some parasols and sacred religious scriptures. The presents came accompanied by a letter in which the King expressed his admiration for the Buddhist doctrine: *"Among all the doctrines, this is the most excellent. It is hard to explain, though, and hard to understand"*. The Japanese reply was along similar lines: *"We have never had the opportunity to listen to such a wonderful doctrine. We do not seem to understand it ourselves either"*.

The emperor gave the image to the head of the Soga clan, so

that he could enjoy it and worship in private. The Soga advocated the spread of Buddhism.

But, with a beginning such as it had, it is easy to understand why Buddhism did not spread straight away. There were also powerful nationalistic forces: two rival factions, the Mononobe and the Nakatomi clans opposed Buddhism and claimed the image had caused a plague. The temple in which the image was housed ended up being burnt and the image of Buddha, thrown into a canal by an enraged mob.

By 857 CE, however, the Soga had their revenge. They annihilated their rivals in battle, built the Hōkōji Temple (The Temple of the Rising Truth), and encouraged the spread of the Buddhist doctrine.

Somehow, Buddhism and Shinto (ancestor worship) learned to coexist. They both remain extremely popular and important to the country.

By the eighth century CE, a monk named Saichō founded Tendai Buddhism. Tendai is a school of Buddhism that incorporates Indian and Chinese traditions. It accepts the unity of all Buddhist schools. Tendai stresses the interconnectedness of all things and the Buddha nature of all beings. Tendai is the school that directly preceded Zen.

Saichō established the headquarters of Tendai in Mount Hiei (Hieizan), near Kyoto. It included three thousand buildings and twenty thousand monks. Unfortunately, the centre was destroyed in 1571. Saichō advocated education and co-operation with the state. As a result, Hieizan became the main Japanese centre of learning.

By the the thirteenth century CE, a monk called Eihei Dōgen, after studying at the monasteries of Hieizan, decides to abandon the teachings of Tendai Buddhism and becomes interested in Zen. The school (that in China was known as *Ch'an*) had been introduced into Japan by another monk, Eisai, who had learnt it in China. Following his steps, Dōgen goes to China, looking for enlightenment. After four years, he becomes enlightened and returns to Japan in 1227.

Throughout his life, Dōgen delivered several sermons that were compiled after his death under the title of *Kana Shōbōgenzō (True Dharma Eye)*. It was written in Japanese, as opposed to other works on *Ch'an*, which were written in Chinese. The legend is that the *Shōbōgenzō* is a distillation of the teachings transmitted by Buddhist Masters going all the way back to Gautama Buddha. The *Shōbōgenzō* refers to the way of awakening, i.e., the Zen way, that is not included in Pali texts. There are several versions of it.

According to some reports, Dōgen's first doubts had to do with training. If we all share the same Buddha Nature, why do we need to practice? He eventually realised what other animal species understand instinctively, you learn to build a nest through practice; you do not ask your parents how to hunt either. You watch, imitate, emulate. Then you become the hunter.

In Japan, Dōgen's methods are extremely successful. Everyone is free to practice Zen. The type of meditation he relied on in order to reach *satori* was *zazen*, which involves sitting cross-legged in silence. He added everyday chores to the practice of Zen. Keeping house, then, becomes a quasi-religious exercise.

With Dōgen's methods, Zen meditation becomes so prevalent in Japan, that it keeps on flourishing today.

In reality—and in line with the total simplification advocated by *Ch'an*—the main method Dōgen chose was to do away with teaching altogether. That was the most important refinement to Gautama Buddha's doctrine. No teaching, no explanation, no words. People who went to his school were forced to find their own ways from the resources of their own character. There was no prayer or ritual to aid them in their quest. All they needed was a zealous spirituality, faith that there was something beyond the self. Then, they had to focus on their meditation to achieve concentration and mindfulness; *satori* would emerge from all that.

True to the principles of Zen, Dōgen rejected all kinds of honours, including a purple robe sent by the Emperor, which he never wore. According to the monk, who by then had founded the Sōtō sect, he didn't need official approval or encouragement; his school of Buddhism was far older than the Kamakura government—he argued—as it had been transmitted by generations of monks, one by one, beginning with Buddha himself.

Sōtō is one of two main Zen schools in Japan. The other one is Rinzai. There are small differences in the way their teachings are conducted, but both essentially maintain the traditions of Zen.

Eventually, Zen Buddhism came to rely on official favour. Emperors sought the advice of monks on many subjects.

Zen monks had a huge impact in Japanese life, not in terms of appealing to the masses, but in changing the habits of the

Japanese higher classes. Many aspects of daily life were influenced by the monks: garden design, the tea ceremony, calligraphy and all types of art and literature became areas where the advice of Zen monks was almost essential.

Musō Soseki, for instance, a thirteenth century Zen master, born within the noble Masamura family, was a renowned poet and calligraphist, but he also became a referential figure in terms of garden design. He had studied the *Shingon* and *Tendai* schools of Buddhism but, after having a dream in which the founder of the *Ch'an* sect in China visited him, he decided to convert to Zen. His gardens include the usual trees, shrubs and greenery, but he also added special features like rocks and raked sand to symbolise the essence of human life, for instance. The intention behind those gardens was for them to encourage meditation. Rock gardens are famous in the West as an easily recognisable element of Zen Buddhism.

Zen Masters in Japan coincided with *Shingon* teachers that *satori* was the most important goal in life; however, following the example of Eisai and Dōgen, they insisted on the highly private and personal nature of enlightenment. Zen acquired its own views, separate from other Buddhist doctrines. The essence of Zen became something to be demonstrated rather than 'taught' in monasteries, in an atmosphere of quiet meditation. Among the main principles that reigned in those monasteries: 1) everyday chores are an important task of spiritual significance, and 2) thinking is useless.

Novices eventually find for themselves that reasoning becomes secondary and intuitive insight takes over. Nobody can reach enlightenment through logic and rationality. Zen cannot be actually taught by means of words—as may happen with other doctrines—it has to be demonstrated, but independent learning is the most important part of the process. Novices have to comprehend Zen by themselves. Nobody can do the learning for them.

So, daily occurrences are important, as is learning without help. Simplicity is one of the main principles of Zen, and that applies to Zen aesthetics as well. Nothing can be baroque, elaborate or artificial. Surrounding oneself with simple things is conducive to feeling, that is part of the philosophy behind rock gardens, or of the blank spaces that are typical of *Suiboku-ga* monochrome ink paintings.

Zen poetry, mainly a type of poem called *haiku*, reflects that simplicity:

The bee emerging from deep within the peony departs reluctantly -Bashō

Like the little stream making its way through the mossy crevices I, too, quietly turn clear and transparent -Ryokan

MOST ZEN MONASTERIES have a big room called the "Meditation Hall", or *zendo*. Monks spend a lot of their time there, as there is where they practice *zazen*, or cross-legged meditation. Each monk has his own space, a *tatami* mat, where he can meditate, and also eat and sleep. Tatami mats are approximately two meters in length by one meter in width. There, monks keep their belongings, which are few.

Each monk has a quilt, but no pillow. When he sleeps, he usually rests his head on his personal effects (robes, a few books, a razor, and some bowls, which he carries in a box). Having or wanting more possessions is considered bad for the spirit.

Meditation is not the main activity in Zen monasteries. Monks have to work. No chore is too menial for them, on the contrary, the lower the task, the better it is for their spiritual life. They have to sweep, scrub, cook, gather timber for fires, till the soil, or go begging in the villages that surround the monastery. No work, no eating. That is part of their philosophy of life. The concept of the working monk was introduced by Hyakujo, a Chinese monk in the eighth century BCE. Hyakujo's idea goes well with the spirit of Zen. Mental work, or any kind of abstract work, has no value for a monk.

Monks have two (sometimes three) meals a day. The meals are frugal, and consist of rice, sometimes mixed with barley, soup and pickled vegetables. Zen, however, does not value asceticism as such. It's just that the monk is supposed to use what he has and not waste anything. After the meal, there should be no grains of rice left in the bowl.

Monks are supposed to lead a simple life, in which humility and poverty are central. That doesn't mean, however, that they cannot enjoy fun or laughter. Their lives are industrious and ordered, and there is no room for useless suffering.

COGNITION, TIME AND IDENTITY

> *"Measured time always presupposes the same inelim-inable fact of experienced duration or temporal passage. In philosophical jargon, duration is an example of 'facticity', something that must be accepted but for which no ground or reason can be given. In Buddhist terms, duration exemplifies 'suchness', a concrete character of being for which no conceptual ground can be given."*
>
> Frank, Gleiser & Thompson - *The Blind Spot*

*I*n the chapter on *Consciousness* we saw that human consciousness includes two discrete layers: sentience and cognition; that they are intertwined and that, the way we are brought up, the layers, or components, can rarely be peeled off. We are born sentient, but cognition is acquired through our parents—especially through our mothers—and through family and society by means of language and culture. It took thousands of years, but eventually cognition acquired an indisputable primacy over sentience: we cannot stop thinking.

Under normal circumstances, the cognitive component really overlaps the senses. Somehow, in our everyday lives, we need to be constantly thinking. It is very difficult to stop. Living in a civilised society requires much more use of cognition than of sentience. In order to survive in our societies, we need a lot of knowledge, a lot of information.

Language and culture give our species clear advantages. Being able to communicate allows us to live in larger groups and create large projects, and we have developed all kinds of innovations through philosophy, science, and technology. Cognition brings many privileges over other animal species, like memory, imagination, creativity and adventurousness. It also gives us measurable time, something other species don't have; they don't have 'time' as a measure of change and, in any case, they cannot measure.

With imagination and time we can think of possible outcomes in the distant future, we can apply strategies to our actions. This involves timescales much longer than those of tactics. Animals can use tactics. Strategies put us several moves in advance. That is why we can play chess, for instance.

Long-term memory means that we are able to create an identity for ourselves that we recognise as our own. Society also accepts that identity of ours. Long-term memory and written language also mean that we can learn not only from our mistakes but from the mistakes of past generations. And we are talking about generations that were gone millennia before our lives.

As we saw, it is easy to think that we *are* our identities, that is, we tend to confuse self-awareness—which is sentient—with identity—which is cognitive. The difference is that identity is something associated with time, whereas self-awareness exists only in the present. In actual fact, we are the present, nothing else.

The rest, when you think about it, appears to be an illusion. But when Zen says it is an illusion, it's saying that what really exists in the now is this person, this you, not the toddler, not the child, or the young person, or the future—older—you. The progression that brought you from toddler, from child, from young person, to the real you right now, however, was something that actually took place. The difference is that only your cognition remembers it.

Your sentience—the biological component of your consciousness—the one that exists right now, the one that can keep you contented and in tune with the universe, does not remember it, the same way the bird does not remember being a chick. The bird just is.

Sentience feels when change is happening. The present is dynamic, change happens from moment to moment. There is a flow that is natural to understand and easy to accept.

Dōgen expresses the flow of time in very simple terms: *'time is being'*. The moment you stop thinking of change in intellectual terms, i.e., in terms of time, the flow has no direction, or is multidirectional, now flows into yesterday and into tomorrow. Now can also flow into now. The amazing thing about it is that the *'I'* that experiences the flow and the flow itself become one. The result is a total selflessness in what Einstein would have called *'time-space'*.

Cognition, on the other hand, analyses change (what it thinks of as 'time') and uses imagination to exacerbate its possibilities. We may want to ignore what is coming, or try to fight it and maintain things as they are, or embrace change—this last option is the one that sentience uses naturally. Many people are anxious about their future and what it will bring. In reality, every choice they make in the present decides what's going to happen to them in the future.

Embracing change means allowing sentience to take over. Meditation makes you more aware of the minute dynamics of change. As you practice mindful meditation, you can feel that everything changes, and become more aware. Any thought-induced feelings of fear, stress, anxiety, or guilt, disappear and become acceptance of the moment.

We have a past because of the incredible development of our long-term episodic memory, and we can also imagine a future: *'In thirty years I will pay my mortgage and be happy; in the meantime, I will have to suffer'*. Zen questions the certainty that we are going to be around in thirty-years time. Do not think about that—it says—concentrate on what's happening now and you will really live. Otherwise, you will spend most of your life expecting some reality that may not come about.

In our daily lives, it is easy, however, to think: 'I have a name. I see things from this perspective. I am separate from the rest of the world. I am this person, I am the same person I was when I was five, and will be the same individual when I am eighty'. But there are differences. If you look at a picture of yours three or four years ago, you will find clear differences. These are noticeable even in very short periods. That identity, that special individual reality that keeps us above the rest of reality and allows us to analyse it, is a product of language and culture (of cognition). Before then, we only had self-awareness. Zen advocates the reintroduction of that natural way of being. Experiencing without overthinking—Zen tells you—is the only way to live a contented life.

But time, as we have seen, is an invention, a construct, that our species has created and uses to great advantage. We superimpose it over a transcendental phenomenon: change. We don't quite understand change, but we have learnt how to measure it. That allows us to plan projects, to manage our daily lives and to live in large societies with other human beings.

What many people don't realise—because it has become second nature to us—is that time does not exist in nature. It's not just that animals do not have the concept of measurable change. Some human cultures don't have it either. And they are not just one or two cases. Here we have mentioned the Pirahã, and the Amondawa in the Amazon basin, the Kuuk Thayorre, in Queensland, Australia, and the Hopi, in Arizona, USA. The fact that time does not exist in nature is not just a supposition. It is a demonstrable reality. Time is like the notion of 'numbers', another human construct.

Without cognition, there are no numbers. Maybe 'one', 'some' and 'many', that's all.

In nature, change comes as a gooey present, a brief moment that flows almost imperceptibly. But we do know that change occurs. And we measure it out of need.

This may sound pedantic to some, but because language is important if we want to convey precise meaning, I would say that perhaps science should introduce a new nomenclature and avoid the unqualified term 'time' as a phenomenon that emerges in a natural state. However, nobody wishes to deny that the concept is absolutely necessary to live in civilised society.

BUT, AND THERE IS A HUGE 'BUT', time brings suffering, having a separate identity brings suffering. All of that has many negative connotations. As we said, we have come to believe that we *are* our identity, that we live within ourselves, when we are really part of the oneness.

Time brings guilt, regret, anxiety, fear: all those feelings are part of suffering. We cannot let go of things or people that we believe are "ours". In reality, nothing is ours.

Time also becomes death. If you think, however, that you are changing constantly, in Buddhist terms you would be constantly being born and dying. Also, if you think that you are one with life itself, experiencing birth and death looses all meaning. Life and death are really the same. Death, rather than being death becomes beyond-death. The enlightened person ceases to fear it. Life and death are something that happen everyday, in your experience and in nature.

A RECENT STUDY conducted at the University of California San Diego claims to have discovered the brain mechanisms behind 'generalised' fear. Generalised fear is the name they give to the fear that appears in the absence of present danger. The study was conducted on mice which, under certain circumstances, received a mild electric shock. The mice developed fear. That fear, however, comes from habituation. Any animal confronted with repetitive threats or incentives—like Pavlov's dogs—develops reactions to those threats or incentives. The difference between those animals and the 'stress-related fear' human beings have is that 'stress-related fear' has to do with time and imagination. We tend to fear the uncertainty of an unknown future. Animals do not suffer that kind of stress. They may have other types of stress, but not one related to fear of what the future may bring. Animals live in the present.

A much more interesting study, this time conducted on humans, established that we prioritise our goals: immediate goals require immediate action (and are recognised faster), whereas future goals are not given priority. The reaction of the hippocampus is located in two different areas. Immediate goals are dealt with in the posterior hippocampus, and future goals, in the anterior one. Our brain appears to have grown in order to accomodate cognition. Not surprisingly, depression-related illnesses are located in the hippocampus.

Cognition is a meta-evolutionary phenomenon that has taken over our lives. We specialise in creating new artificial habits. Right now we are into cell phones, tablets, laptops and all kinds of other paraphernalia that make us believe we live in the future. Long before those devices existed, we allowed overthinking to become our habit and our master. The result is that our senses are almost dormant. We do things in a hurry. We multitask. We expect to finish that task to reach the end, the completion that is going to make us happy. Instead—Zen says—we should enjoy the *doing*.

So, we normally see ourselves as separate from the rest of reality, and we act within a 'time' that involves long-term memory and long-term imagination. All of this is artificial. Zen rejects this 'false' reality, but it is not just a rejection. It's the acceptance of a new reality. When the Zen practitioner attains immediate awakening, it is not based on normal rejection of anything, or normal affirming, which means accepting a 'within' and a 'without'.

The true insight of the enlightened is the negation of all things and acceptance of the Dharma. Sentience—which we already have because it comes with our birth—needs to be acknowledged as the true reality. Focusing on the present and rejecting our apparent separation with the rest of reality is the only answer. The moment we accept reality as it is—which does not *include* us, because we *are* reality—we enter 'the zone'. There is an energy that comes from within and is the bond we have with reality. Reality, then, is a timeless state in which we become our pure origins.

We can feel the wisdom that knows no suffering, and we can focus on *being* and *doing*, which are one and the same. You have sentience within you—Zen tells you—and that is the answer to your quest for wisdom, for enlightenment. That *within* is also *without*. You are oneness.

SENTIENCE AND SELF-AWARENESS

"An intrinsic property is traditionally understood as a property that something would have even if it were the only thing in the universe or the only thing in existence. Does that idea even make sense? Not if you think that something is what it is only by virtue of its belonging to a web of relations. Why not say that relations determine the occupants of the relations, after the fashion of relational quantum mechanics? Or that relations and occupants are mutually interdependent?"

Frank, Gleiser & Thompson - *The Blind Spot*

"The over-all number of minds is just one. I venture to call it indestructible since it has a peculiar timetable, namely mind is always now. There is really no before

and after for mind. There is only a now that includes memories and expectations."

Erwin Schrödinger - *What is life?*

What we have seen in previous chapters is that the West has been fascinated by Eastern cultures ever since it established contact with them. That fascination has always been somewhat superficial, because a real understanding of the East requires a profound change of perspective.

It would be easy to fall into a gross oversimplification of the situation, but I will try to make it as simple as possible without ovesimplifying: normally, the idea is that, in the West, the individual is totally independent from the reality that surrounds him or her, and that, in the East, the individual is completely interdependent with the rest of society and with nature. Reality is a tad more complicated than that.

As we have seen, consciousness has two layers: one is sentience and the other one, cognition. Sentience is biological, or physical (that is, we are born with it), whereas cognition is metaphysical (it is acquired through the culture).

Traditionally, the West has considered that the self—how the individual perceives him or herself—is meta-cognitive, that is, that the self resides in a metaphysical consciousness. A great deal of that perception has to do with the Cartesian dictum *"Cogito ergo sum"* or *"Je pense donc je suis"*, where Descartes appears to be saying: *"Without thought there is no self"*. In any case, he does not say that. That is the way it has been interpreted. It would be possible to explain it philosophically, but it would really be digressing big time.

The other problem is that, often, Western philosophy and science take 'self-awareness' and 'identity' as interchangeable concepts when, in reality, self-awareness and identity have totally different natures. There is a reason for it. We acquire a "self" the moment we are born. We become ourselves when we are sentient. The self, as we shall see, resides in the present. On the other hand, our identity lives in time and requires long-term memory and imagination; both of those elements are cognitive: they are acquired through the collective and the culture.

Eastern philosophies have worked out that difference: in the East—for Zen, among other disciplines—the self resides in the body, the self is part of sentience alone.

IF THE READER would allow me a bit of self-reference again, I can say that I have suffered from transient amnesia and have first-hand experience of the fact that you can be conscious without knowing who you are; but you are still self-aware—otherwise you would not be conscious. You can feel that you exist (and you don't have to prove it by thinking). In that respect, I find that my direct experience tends to corroborate what Eastern philosophies affirm is real.

Often, you lose your memory because you lose your cognition (lose your mind?) As we explained, without cognition,

SENTIENCE AND SELF-AWARENESS

time does not exist. To make it clearer, let me explain what happened to me when I had the first episode of transient amnesia: I woke up one morning without remembering who I was (but I was sure I existed). I had a self but no identity. The questions I asked myself, which I recall quite clearly, were: "Where am I?"; "Is this my house?" (I knew 'house'); "Who is this woman lying next to me?"; "Is she my wife? (I knew 'wife')". The absence lasted a few minutes. I told my wife and we both laughed. We thought I had not been quite awake. The episodes, however, reoccurred on other occasions in the middle of the day.

Self-awareness is biological and present, whereas identity is hybrid, i.e., metaphysical and cultural (therefore time-related). You are self-aware the moment you are conscious, regardless of being alone or with other people. Self-awareness occurs only in the present; you cannot be self-aware in the past or in the future. You can remember, imagine or dream being self-aware, though.

Identity, on the other hand, is cultural and metaphysical because you acquire it through the collective. A tiger does not have an identity. Maybe elephants or whales have a semblance of identity because they live in groups. We don't know.

In reality, you have within you a much longer, underlying memory. It's the genetic signature of all your ancestors. In scientific terms it is called deoxyribonucleic acid, or DNA. But that long, long-term memory has little to do with you as an individual, or with cultural or national identity. Your DNA is the biological stamp of who you are and, far from being individual, it carries with it the other side, the complementary part of nature, the part that you cannot see or understand. You are unique and, at the same time, your DNA proves the physical contribution of all those other beings that make you who you are. Some of them are dead, some of them might still be alive. Some other people who partially share your DNA probably live in remote places and there are many you do not even know.

Human beings have identities because identities are necessary to function within their social groups. The time-related aspect of one's identity has to do with the continuity of that identity through the name society gives the individual. Normally, identity is permanent. For the individual and for society. It may vary in the case of a change of name, or marriage, or gender change, but those are only socially accepted exceptions.

I would like to emphasise and reinforce these concepts as they are extremely important: bodily self-awareness occurs solely in the present and is part of sentience. The cognitive self (identity)—as experienced in long-term episodic memory and anticipation (past and future)—is obviously part of cognition, and, like time, it is only a human construct. Other species have neither long-term episodic memory nor anticipation (at least they do not appear to imagine long-term into the future). They have associative memory only. There have been many cases of dogs, or other pets, that keep on waiting for their humans to return because they cannot imagine the possibility of a permanent absence.

The self as a personal storyline—as a biography, let's say—is

SENTIENCE AND SELF-AWARENESS

what you know as your identity; it happens in time and within the collective.

If we understand, then, that identity is not really self, if we understand that it owes its existence to the collective and to cognition, we can also say that identity is as non-existent as time. They are both creations of the human mind. They are both constructs that help you live in society. Actually, your past life was something that really took place, and change also occurred. It's just that only your long-term memory remembers it. Your actual self is now. A hawk does not remember her childhood, let's put it that way.

Being present, according to Zen, for instance, is being in a state of pure sentience. There is no thought and no shallow form. The outer body is important, but not as important as the inner one. The inner body is one with nature, which is wordless and thoughtless. The difference with Christianity —in which the divine is equated with *"the Verb"*—is diametrical and quite evident. Feelings and sensations, according to Zen, connect you to the truth. Being present, then, is the atavistic return to our origins, to the pure nature of our ancestors.

Current human beings are the product of a meta-evolutionary leap that occurred when we started using language. As we said before, the first instance of a phoneme marks the onset of humanity. We became human only when an individual understood the meaning another individual was trying to convey by means of sound.

That was an incredible advance, a leap into the unknown. In many ways, what came after that was something totally artificial, that other species do not have.

H. sapiens, unwittingly, was adding a layer to consciousness that would place the species in a perhaps enviable but sometimes difficult situation.

When I say meta-evolutionary, I mean that our exponential advance in terms of collective institutions and technology did not abide by any of the natural rules of evolution and survival of the fittest that were discovered by Charles Darwin, and that otherwise applied to all other species. Russel Wallace knew it and Darwin suspected it. Our societies are anything but natural. Our institutions are invented, they are constructs.

We have acquired a consciousness, a self, an ego, an imagination. We have acquired time and also isolated ourselves from nature. We believe that we are our individual consciousness —and our identity. But it is the other way around. The collective imposes that identity on our self.

HERE WE CANNOT HELP but returning to Heraclitus, the river is the same and the individual is the same. How? To some extent they are both different, pretty much like the ship of Theseus: components gradually change. The secret of the continuity is the day-by-day imperceptibility of that change.

In the case of the Greek myth, all the planks of the ship, which was normally docked at the port of Athens, slowly rotted away and were replaced, one by one. The ship was real and change was real. At the end, however, the ship was not quite the same, except in people's perception. Apart from the paradox in terms of identity, the ship was involved in a myth but was also part of real history. The execution of Socrates, had to be delayed because no execution could be carried out while the ship was not in port.

THERE IS nothing as atavistic and distant in history as our DNA but it is still part of our real selves.

To summarise, none of the cells that make up your body are the same as the cells your body had when you were one year old. None. All of your cells change every seven years. And yet, after you were born, you were given a name and you feel you are the same person as that newborn baby. Your DNA is the same, and your family and friends perceive you as the same person. But there's something illusory about that sameness. You have memories and have acquired experience. All of that came through the big leap our species took when humans became conscious; in reality, your actual self is the physical person you are now, and only that person.

As soon as you realise that your self is just your bodily self, and that it only exists in the present, then it is much easier to comprehend that you are as much reality as the sky is.

The opposite would be thinking that you are separate from reality, that you have intrinsic properties, that is, properties that you would have if you were the only thing in the universe. That does not make a lot of sense. Something (or someone) is what or who that being is by virtue of their relations with other entities. Some Buddhist sects reject even the existence of intrinsic properties; currently, quantum physicists and some Western philosophers agree with them on the primacy of relations over entities. The observer and the observed, remember?

Let's say you look at the sky, you have a sensation of it. You are using your eyes to see it. But when you think that you are part of that reality as well, the difference between you and the sky disappears. You don't have a sensation of the sky. You are not really that separate, you are not apart from the sky. You are part of what you sense and you feel. You begin to feel the sky as identical to your life, as the seagull or the jaguar do. They don't remember what happened to them when they were five years old. Only humans remember episodes of our past. Only our species can imagine what could happen to us in the future.

LET us go back to self-awareness and the East. In Japanese culture, among other Asian cultures, the notion of the self is closer to that of an 'embodied mind'. That way, it is much easier to understand that the self does not come from self-reflection, it has nothing to do with thinking. And I state this with all due respect to Descartes,—who used *"I think"* to prove existence but did not discard the possibility of existence without thought.

In Japanese culture, then, the self has to do with being, with agency in the real world. Identity is a different thing, as we have already seen.

The confusion in Western philosophy and science, rather than coming from rejecting Cartesian substance duality (mind as opposed to body)—which they do—, comes from not accepting that there is a duality in consciousness itself.

Once we have grasped that in Japanese culture the self is part of sentience, not of cognition, it becomes easier to understand how Zen views the self: it has nothing to do with thinking but with being able to act in the real world. Human individuals exist in an environment that enables them to do what they do. The individual is not an island, it is integrated in nature and society. Intersubjectiveness, remember?

In the West, the existence of the self relies on identity and individuality, and it is considered an internal phenomenon. That concept includes an activity—the pronoun "I"—that knows the self, and a passivity—the pronoun "me"—which is the self that is known. In the West, the self appears to exist through self-reflection.

In the East, the (interdependent) self knows that its existence draws upon social and natural relationships without which it would not be there. The individual is connected to, and highly conditioned by, the environment.

This is reflected in Japanese pronouns like 私 (*watashi*), which is the same as 私 (*watakushi*), formal; あたし (*atashi*), for females; おれ (*ore*) and 僕 (*boku*), for males, all of which are equivalent to "I", but in different social situations.

あなた (*anata*) which is the equivalent of second person "you" in English, is not as used as much, and it appears to be etymologically related to "*anatta*" in Sanskrit, which means "that which is not I".

At first it would seem, then, that in Japanese, the self is not sustained by an internal view, but it is the opposite: a phenomenon conditioned by external perception. Actually, it is something even more subtle, as we saw with "anata", there is rather a relationship between "self" and "no-self". The self is based on its interaction with the rest of reality, with the environment.

The individual, of course, remains the individual. Only the relationship is different. There is an inner component, where true motives lie, and an outer component of that reality, expressed by the way the Japanese speaker adapts to the social world.

What Western/ Greek/ Christian objective reality does is it takes away our participatory wholeness, the wholeness we should have with the rest of reality. This is not meant as criticism, it's just the way things are. The moment we observe something we cease to be part of it. We cannot experience that something. But the person who understands, the person who has attained wisdom to some degree, does not go around thinking that he or she *"is reality"*. Reality simply *"is"* and the person is integrated in it.

The sentient self, then, is united with the rest of nature. It experiences.

As we mentioned before, at one point in the evolution of our species, cognition was superimposed on sentience. It is a layer; an artificial layer at that. Once you understand that cognition—thought—is the smaller component of consciousness that has taken over, you realise that all the beauty and the peace lie somewhere else. All the important things in life are in a natural environment that exists beyond cognition.

CONCLUSION

"How difficult and how misleading it would be to try and understand Zen literally and logically ... Of course, so far as they are given as answers they are pointers by which we may know where to look for the presence of the Buddha; but we must remember that the finger pointing at the moon remains a finger and under no circumstances can it be changed into the moon itself. Danger always lurks where the intellect slyly creeps in and takes the index for the moon itself."

D.T. Suzuki - *An Introduction to Zen Buddhism*

" 'Those guys got high on nothing, hey?' 'Sip your tea and you'll see; this is good green tea'. It was good and I immediately felt calm and warm.

CONCLUSION

> '*Want me to read you parts of this Han Shan poem? Want me to tell you about Han Shan?*'
>
> '*Yeah*'
>
> '*Han Shan you see was a Chinese Scholar who got sick of the big city and took off to hide in the mountains*' "

Jack Kerouac - *The Dharma Bums*

> "... *There's nothin' behind me and nothin' that ties me*
>
> *To somethin' that might have been true yesterday*
>
> *Tomorrow is open and right now it seems to be more*
>
> *Than enough to just be here today*
>
> *And I don't know what the future is holdin' in store*
>
> *I don't know where I'm goin', I'm not sure where I've been*
>
> *There's a spirit that guides me, a light that shines for me*
>
> *My life is worth the livin', I don't need to see the end*
>
> *Sweet, sweet surrender*
>
> *Live, live without care*
>
> *Like a fish in the water*
>
> *Like a bird in the air.*"

John Denver - *Sweet Surrender*

CONCLUSION

In the *Introduction* I quoted D.T. Suzuki and said that, although he is correct in his statement to the effect that Zen is impossible to understand using normal logic, I would try and do exactly that. Here I repeat the process with a similar quotation. There is a clear caveat, though: this book does not give you a recipe for enlightenment. It only explains how the process works and provides extra information for you to put that process into context. If you want to pursue the idea of Zen and *satori*, you will have to go through the experience yourself. Nobody else can do it for you.

What Suzuki and other Masters say about Zen is true to some extent, "... *the finger pointing at the moon remains a finger and under no circumstances can it be changed into the moon itself...*". However, unless we observe the moon and question why it is a full moon, or why it is surrounded by mist, or why during the day it disappears from view, we will never understand that, while our finger remains with us, the moon goes around the planet.

Also, I believe most Westerners interested in Zen find that there is a mystery that frustrates them no end. They are afraid that they are getting married and don't know their partner. Love is good, but before you get married you need to know something about the other person. Faith is also good, but sometimes it's not enough.

For those who have skipped to this *Conclusion*, let me state plainly: attaining enlightenment, *nirvana* or *satori*, involves

CONCLUSION

discarding every thought that may come to your mind, and enhancing innate sentience through total focus on the present moment via meditation.

We explained before that the existential and intellectual components—or layers—of human consciousness have become so enmeshed in us, after hundreds of thousands of years, that it seems almost impossible to peel one of them off. This is where Zen meditation holds its secret: gradually dissolving cognition, thereby exponentially heightening sentience.

Zen also appears to prove that, if you are able to separate the components of human consciousness that are so difficult to study as a whole, it must be because their natures are different. While sentience's physical basis in neurones and synapses is undeniable, many aspects of our intellect—both individual and collective—hint at an intangible nature beyond physical sciences' grasp.

We live thinking about the future. We regret big chunks of our lives and blame ourselves for all kinds of failures. We are not rich, we are not famous, we are not successful, and even if we are, we're still unhappy. What Gautama Buddha said about suffering is a reality for billions of human beings. They have patterns of behaviour they cannot leave behind. They live dull and often unproductive lives. Things do not need to be like that.

Maybe you complain or judge. '*The situation I'm in right now is unbearable*', you might say. Then, perhaps you should go away. *'I have to deal with this person at work that makes my life really difficult'*. Then you should do something about it. You can resign and find another job, you can talk to their boss, or accept the situation and live with it (move away from it, change it, or accept it).

When you focus your life in the present, you realise that those problems do not exist. They are either in your imagination (you expect people to act in certain ways), in the past, or in the future. Being in a situation that you consider stressful or unhappy means you really don't want to be in that situation. Complaining does not solve it. You have to get rid of that situation and move to a present where you are happy. It's like complaining that you should have done something that you did not do. Or the other way around, that you did something that you shouldn't have done. Complaining is not going to change the past. Forget it. It's done. As we said before, animals have no 'should'. Sentience has no 'should'.

Perhaps you are waiting to be rich. That will not happen by magic in the future. To be rich or prosperous you have to do something about it, and that happens in the present, in the now. A journey of ten thousand miles commences with the first step, and the only step that matters is the one you take now. Ultimately—Zen advises—being in the present means figuring out that there *are* no problems.

What Masters like Dōgen tell you is that, practising Zen meditation and applying it to your daily life, at a certain point you will experience '*oneness*'. Furthermore, Dōgen assures that the moment you begin to meditate you will experience something he calls '*luminosity*'. That is, the moment you realise that the activities of your body and of

CONCLUSION

your mind are not separate activities, you gain an incredible insight, and that happens during your meditation. When he says '*mind*', I am certain he is actually saying that your body and your senses are one and the same. During meditation, your 'self' (your identity, not self-awareness) begins to disappear, he says. Then, your body and your mind '*drop away*'.

What cannot be explained in words, what does not have any logic during those moments, is that the person who bows to you and you become one; there are no measures or distances; things that are large become small, and vice versa, a speck of dust becomes the moon. And that, however, does not mean that reality has changed. It just means that your perspective of it is different.

That is also what happens the moment you are creating. You do not depend on the result. You don't expect a result. You enjoy the moment. You hope your painting will be good, but it doesn't matter if it isn't. You do not expect ecstatic comments from critics, neither are you leaving your painting to posterity. The act of painting is great regardless of what happens after the act of creation takes place. Many people do not understand this. You love doing it just because you enjoy *being* creative. If the work wins an award, that is great too, but that was not the point of the creation.

It is clear that the hawk does not think when she is hunting, she *is* the hunt. Her decisions may be described as 'thoughtless' because—unlike humans—she does not need to think, nor does she have the capacity to do it. Her actions are perfected by experience and backed up by the evolution, instincts, and habits acquired through thousands of generations of hawks before her. All her senses are fully integrated with what is happening that very moment. As she faces the possibility of a hunt, her senses are enhanced, her reflexes are perfect.

Somehow, 'thoughtless' is a word that, in modern cultures, has acquired negative connotations. That is because, in these cultures, the intellect is considered more important than the senses.

We know an impala is not distracted by the beauty of the colour green when he is running. He just *runs*. His concentration is boundless because it cannot be otherwise. He is the part of the whole that is moving, exactly like his predator moves. He *is* nature. And he survives or dies *being* it.

Those animals are sentient beings, they are an integral part of nature, if you like. Reality encompasses them. Paradoxically, they and the rest of the world (*"anatta"* in Sanskrit—that which is not them) are really one. There is a self and a non-self which complement each other perfectly. It is not just them and the outside of their 'selves' as we would think in the West. Reality is not objective, it's only reality. And it *includes* them. Predator and prey are, in that reality, one. They could not exist without each other. The predator is defined by the prey and vice versa. The fox cannot exist without the rabbit and the rabbit would probably multiply itself to extinction without the fox. And there is no logic to it. Zen tells us that anything to do with logic is something we

CONCLUSION

add to our analysis in order to understand something that needs no understanding. Things are the way they are.

Those selves are that environment and those circumstances (we can think of space and time, if you like; but for them there is only fluid present and change). The moment is brief. Some species may have long-term affective memory, but they do not have long-term episodic memory. They may have present fear or anger; what they do not have is anxiety or stress. In humans, these latter feelings are acquired, they are the product of thought. Anxiety, for instance, is fear of something that might happen in the future. Many things cause anxiety. We are anxious about the possibility of failure in love, or at work, or in an exam situation. If there is real danger, though—Zen assures us—sentience takes over. One acts according to instinct. One either fights or flees.

Stress comes from not being able to cope with a situation that is not quite what the individual had expected. Both anxiety and stress, as we said, have to do with cognition. They do not exist without time.

Animals, instead, will only deal with the future when it becomes present, when real things occur, not with future possibilities. They have no regrets or guilt either. The past is gone. Whatever they do is what they need to do.

They act according to the environment and within the circumstances. They are also the action and the change. There is no good or evil. A lion hunts when she is hungry herself or needs to feed her cubs. Killing her prey is just part of what she has to do to continue living, which is her instinct.

In the same way—for the animal— maybe there is no ugliness or beauty in anything, we don't know. There is no judgement, only acceptance, because of its inclusion in the whole. He accepts nature because he *is* nature. He cannot do otherwise.

Of course, there is a germ of cognition in some species. Our cognition must have evolved from somewhere. Theirs is not as highly developed as ours is nowadays. Human cognition has developed through millennia of complex language, communication and thought; and it continues developing with every generation. Other species have communication and probably some kind of language, not complex, and definitely not recursive, like ours. Still, the animal species that have sentient agency operate perfectly within the here and the now of nature.

Similarly (but only similarly), when a buddhist monk reaches *satori* (which is, as you have gathered, pure sentience), he empties his mind from cognition, he *becomes* reality in a human but ineffable way; he does not witness what is happening because he *is* part of that dynamics; like a jaguar or a starling, he *becomes* the activity. The action (or non-action) cannot be explained because it cannot be understood by means of thought. It needs no words. Thus, it is ineffable.

What we are trying to give you, however, is not quite a repeat of the experience, but a description, like the guy describing the painting by Van Gogh. What you get is an approximation, enough to give you an idea of what monks do and why they do it.

CONCLUSION

But let's go back... The monk, then, *is* the garden, or the flower, or the arrow. He empirically understands reality, he 'lives' it. The Zen experience—non-solipsistic as it is—reaches its goal, but it is an indescribable goal, which the cognitive component of the mind finds difficult to comprehend, and the Western mind finds even difficult to accept. It is something that the Zen teacher cannot explain either. He can only demonstrate. That is the reason (our Western reasoning) behind the lack of logic, and the fact that words are not an acceptable way of teaching. The *sensei*, or teacher, can only show the way.

One beautiful—and normally true—meaning of the word - せんせい (*"sensei"*) is that, when written in *kanji*, it includes the roots 先 (*"sen"*) "before" and 生 ("sei") "life". That is, the teacher is someone who's born before the student. An elder, a wiser person.

The moment the monk practices, he lets go of cognition, he lets go of the past and the future. That moment, he *becomes* a total awareness of his body. That moment, he does not have an ego, an identity or a biographical history. He *is* the moment. He chooses to be that natural something that is timelessness. He becomes one with nature and change. An interesting aspect of becoming a Zen monk is the loss of any former identity: names are not important any more. He may be given a new name, but you will see that *koans* rarely use names. Names have to do with identity and thus with time.

People who meditate, even before becoming enlightened, focus on their sentience; what happens is that all of their senses become totally enhanced, as much as they can be. Some want to believe that *satori* is something like a drug-induced trance. In reality there is no trance. The person is completely alert. What the person that reaches *satori* has achieved is total unity with nature. He or she retains the self but is in a position where he or she becomes the nature that encompasses that self, that includes it: the here and now. Oneness.

Only the artificial, meta-evolutionary, component of consciousness is set aside, or is kept in the background. *Satori*, then, is an intense awareness, a highly satisfying sensation. You have almost no cognition but are alert. You reach the very essence of each moment. There is no suffering, just a feeling of satisfaction with what you do. And joy. That may include creativity or merely being.

Do we know what it would be like to experience the world without cognition, the way our hominin ancestors did? We can only speculate. The thing is, we do not need to go back to that stage, and neither do we need to copy other species. Often you hear Zen Masters talking about the 'original mind', but they don't mean going back all the way to not being human. By leaving cognition behind us, all we are doing is advancing towards enlightenment.

Meditation is consciousness minus overthinking. What Zen advocates is not to allow cognition to take over—as most people do—because that comes with negative feelings and suffering. But we can still use it, only in a more effective fashion. As we said, the person who meditates, or the enlightened person, becomes immensely focused because he or she *is* the moment. There is no negativity of any kind. It is exactly the opposite: negativity comes with cognition, but

CONCLUSION

especially with overthinking. What happens with *satori* is total acceptance.

Cognition and sentience, we repeat, are essential modules of the current conscious structure of our species. They are discrete but integrated; they cannot be peeled off. However, through Zen meditation, the negative aspects of cognition are set aside.

Satori is not just about the attainment of wisdom. It means a seamless integration with reality. As explained, all senses are enhanced. It is a joyful epiphany. Sudden enlightenment implies the discovery of a totally new experience. The real world has different colours, smells and sensations. Everything is intense.

Because we are normally in a cognitive mode, it is easy to think of enlightenment as something incredible and beyond us. Luckily, it is the natural state in which we are supposed to be (in which we were before language and culture). It happens all of a sudden: a revelation. Maybe immediately, maybe after years of meditation. Practice becomes experience, and experience is sentience. One day, the Zen student finds himself or herself in a special place, in 'the zone', without even trying. And he or she can stretch that moment at will.

What is also immensely satisfying is the realisation that us, as human beings are not actually separated from reality. It is the realisation that separation is just an illusion, something that was brought about by the intellect. What is real is the connection with the world around us, the discovery that we *are* it. What Gautama Buddha promised is that the moment you reach that stage there is no more suffering.

And it does not mean regressing to our hominin past either. A *H. sapiens* individual will always remain a full human being. Before our prolonged leap into full human cognition, we had the innate facility of pure animal sentience. Well, this is exactly that: the revival of that full sentience, but we now can achieve that without losing our capacity to think at will.

Also—with the practice of Zen—the presence of ethics and morals will always remain there. What is attained is full integration with nature and with society through sentience. There is peace and there is acceptance.

What disappears at the moment of enlightenment are the intellectual components that are negative. One of them, as we explained, is time. Fear of anything that might happen in the future disappears with it. When you are in the present, you do not think of dying. Before, I said that animals are iterations of their species. And we are iterations of ours. Animals are immortal because they do not think of dying. One of the warnings of God to Adam and Eve when he told them not to eat of the 'tree of knowledge of good and evil', was that 'if you do, you will surely die'. Of course, He did not mean that literally, and they didn't die, but He was not wrong. As the proto-humans they were, they were immortal, but the moment they knew they would eventually die, they became mortal.

Let's emphasise what we said in the chapter on *Consciousness:* we mentioned that time resides in the cognitive component of human consciousness. Animals don't wear watches, nor do they have any idea of time. They only know change, like our ancestors did. Our species became preoccupied with time when we passed from understanding seasons and days

CONCLUSION

to studying the movement of celestial bodies and predicting phenomena like tides and eclipses. Then, humans needed to measure change. We came up with all sorts of measuring devices like clepsydras and candle clocks. The invention of mechanical clocks in Europe quickly gave rise to pocket watches. Now we have atomic clocks that can almost measure Planck time, the tiniest measure of time scientists can imagine. We also enjoy smart watches that help us in all sorts of new ways within our social life.

It's not just that with meditation time disappears, even the notion of time disappears. You concentrate on anything that is happening in the present. The result is that your senses are enhanced and you walk into 'the zone'. The moment you let go of thought, as we said, you let go of the idea of time as well. Your senses have no room for time.

Living in the past brings nostalgia, regret, shame, and guilt, among other feelings that only obstruct and mean suffering. Thinking about the future often comes at the cost of ignoring the present. There is fear of what might happen, and that brings non-acceptance of change. The future brings anxiety and stress. So long as we are using both our sentient-self and our cognitive-self together, we have conflict, tension, fear. (The sentient self by itself is free. It lives totally, and that brings with it a feeling of fulfilment). The tension comes because the components of our human consciousness have different natures: sentience evolved naturally, cognition is meta-evolutionary (when you think about it, it is so artificial that it has to be taught, again and again, to each generation).

Buddhism—Zen, in particular—is the present. The Zen practitioner, the monk, tries to live in the present as much as possible. There is nothing else. There are no thoughts, no distractions. Only the task at hand. And when the senses are enhanced, that task is a joy to perform and will be completed to perfection.

Gautama Buddha came up with an amazing notion as a result of his rejection of the evils of civilisation. His philosophy, however, became misunderstood and grew into different schools or sects of Buddhism. Zen is the return to basics. No teaching. Only experience—doing—takes you there.

When a Zen practitioner creates anything—like anyone who experiences the 'flow', or is 'in the zone' (as we sometimes call the moment we are creating something)—, he or she retains a very important sensation: かんそ ("kanso"), "feeling". The Zen practitioner is aware of what's going on, but there is no actual plan, there is no overthinking or strategy about further moves, there is no effort, only momentum. Creation is pure joy. It flows.

Zen art includes anything from pottery, gardening, calligraphy, kendo—or any of the Japanese martial arts—and is renowned the world over.

One famous Zen artist, Kazuaki Tanahashi, specialises in calligraphy, but is also an author and painter. Tanahashi discovered Zen in the nineteen-sixties, when he met Zen master Soichi Nakamura. Together, they translated Dōgen's *Shōbōgenzō* into modern Japanese, which they published in the early 1970s. Tanahashi, who is currently 91 years old, is still working on his next book. He believes *"Death is always beside us... Death is always faithful with you."* Dying, he believes, should produce a sense of gratitude in us. What better way to describe the influence of Zen on an individual?

CONCLUSION

The moment, like everything that happens in the world of Zen, as we have said several times, is now, in the present; that is, things are happening. There is another important consideration: ここ (*"koko"*) "here". Wherever the person is, that is where things happen. Nowhere else. Nothing else is important. Only now, and only here. Total sentience.

Other feelings form part of the experience; there is a great sensation that things are happening the way they have to happen: しぜん (*"shizen"*) "naturalness", and that the moment is a special one, it is not done out of habit: だいすぞく ("daisuzoku") "non-routine".

All of that translates into a sensation: ゆげん (*"yugen"*) that can only be described as "a deep state of grace, or mysteriousness". That is what you can expect when—even if momentarily—you discard your thoughts.

One lovely discovery I made is that ここ (*"koko"*), which means "here", as we said, is included in こころ (*"kokoro"*), which also means "mind" as well as "heart", written in *kanji* as 心 (*"kokoro"*). Both, 'heart' and 'mind', include 'here'. That also gives us an idea of the differences between East and West in terms of language and culture.

Western scholars have confirmed that more experienced jazz musicians can improvise better and enjoy the process more than musicians that have practised less. What happens when musicians improvise is the unplanned flow—as the name implies—of music. Pure creation.

When I mention experience, I mean people who have practised more. The process of practice involves eventually doing things without thinking. Improvising music requires skills that are acquired only through habit. The senses are enhanced. It could be like riding a bicycle, playing the piano, or touch-typing. You do it without actually thinking. It's something that has become second nature. It is totally intuitive. You are the hunter and the prey, you are the instrument and you are the music. Art in general—and not only music —relies on practice.

Zen encourages the practice of meditation because it allows the novice to acquire experience; during that time, the senses take over from the intellect. When artists create, they do it in a situation of mental stillness. Experience becomes expertise. And expertise allows the Zen master to induce a state of concentration and relaxation that becomes total integration with the here and now. That brings non-self, contentment, acceptance, and very often, joy. Acceptance of the oneness with nature is something essential. When we let go, we go with the flow of that very nature. The moment we accept and stop fighting with what we are doing, we become what we are doing. Acceptance means not opposing what is happening.

Life is not always creation. Real life includes the drudgery of daily domestic chores; and, when we concentrate on the task at hand, even that experience can be enjoyable. We quoted before that famous saying *"Before satori, chopping wood and carrying water; after satori, chopping wood and carrying*

CONCLUSION

water". That is what Dōgen taught. Among other things, wisdom means acceptance of everyday necessities.

In this respect, Japanese Buddhism differs from Indian Buddhism, in which idleness is an acceptable form of meditation. Zen promotes industriousness.

Before, we said that ideas are different from thoughts. That requires a separate explanation. Sometimes we see the symbol of a lightbulb to indicate a new idea. New ideas are part of an actual *process* of innovation. They can occur with minimal thinking. Sentience does it for you.

Creativity and innovation appear the moment sentience meets cognition. How does that happen? We might have a problem at work, or we have an assignment, or have to write an essay. The ideas are not forthcoming, there is no flow. One of the ways out of it is to 'sleep on it'. The following morning we often find that we have solved the problem.

Sometimes we are slowly waking up from a dream—more often than not, a fairly lucid dream—and the solution has come to us. The moment you're dreaming or beginning to wake up from the dream, there is no reasoning. Dreams are never logical. You are still pure sentience, and even without knowing it, you already have the solution. You are beginning to wake up. That is the moment when the transfer occurs. You begin to think. The cognitive component of your consciousness receives the solution from somewhere. There is an inner energy; without thought there is a special kind of stillness. That is the lightbulb moment, and that often

CONCLUSION

happens to anybody who's coming out of a dream and yet enjoying the incredible benefit of full sentience.

Another instance of that, let's say, is when you are creating music or painting, or doing something in the visual arts. Emotion is involved and, again, that is when sentience meets cognition. The emotion flows into the canvas, or the metal, or the music. And the spectator, or the audience, can share in the feeling; they can identify with the artist. That is when the real magic occurs. Very often you feel the painting has painted itself, and you have been some kind of intermediary.

The thought that takes place before creation is something that occurs in the mind. The emotion, on the other hand is, more or less, physical. The artist has it when he or she is creating, and the public receives it the moment it is seeing it or listening to it. It flows like a river, and it keeps on flowing regardless of when the creation took place. The emotion is in the now, in the present, with all senses enhanced by what is happening. Art is a form of communication that overpowers the intellect. Life could also be a form of art if you choose it to be so. There is no need to remember or imagine anything. There is no award. There should be no award. Painting is the enjoyment of painting without any thought about the future or anything else.

You meditate—or you are enlightened—; you don't need to be asleep to enjoy full sentience. The acceptance that you are in a situation of oneness with reality brings the stillness you need, and, as you don't have constant interruptions, as you don't have the background noise coming from your thoughts... wham!, solutions to problems, and art, come without thinking. There is no secret there. You are not sepa-

CONCLUSION

rate, on the contrary, you are perfectly in tune with the world and the universe.

∾

Before the Table of Contents of this book there are some texts that are difficult to explain. They have no logic. Well, there is no logic in Zen. Thinking that life has to be logical is what is expected. We normally think that life has a trajectory, and that that trajectory should be dictated by logic; we have been brought up to expect that. Those are rules that are imposed on us by thought. Zen's rejection of logic comes with the package. No thought.

Accepting something that has no logic to it is the beginning of liberation. The moment you reject the logic that is imposed upon you, you begin to attain wholeness. Your mental and physical components are there. You have a body and you have a mind, but you are neither. You are the whole, and that whole is 'part of' (or actually *is*) something much, much bigger: oneness. Without the rest of reality you would not exist. You are a drop in the ocean, but the drop *is* the ocean. Without drops there would not be any ocean and without the ocean, the drops would be nothing.

That 'oneness' is what is impossible to understand intellectually. Your cognition will try to analyse and give names. 'Oneness', however, is not there to be analysed. It just *is*. To put it in terms we can understand better, it is 'eternal' (it has no time) and infinite (it has no end). Oneness exists, if you like, in time and space.

CONCLUSION

The only way to transcend cognition is letting go, accepting that reality does not need you to judge it, and judging it does not give you anything in return. Cognition analyses everything, it needs to question in order to understand. Cognition is inquisitive. Sentience accepts. It is much more powerful. If you want to, you can think of sentience in biblical terms: it is *nephesh* ("the breath of life"). Sentience is life, pretty much like you, with your senses, symbolise living.

What I am trying to explain here is the process involved. By now, I'm sure you have gathered that much.

Being in the present requires pure sentience, which is not actually total consciousness. It requires abstaining from the normal way humans analyse situations and think. It requires putting cognition in the back burner.

Being in the present is assuming there is something that is not obvious, something that can be 'demonstrated', like Zen does, but not normally 'explained'. This book is explaining it, and it includes a more detailed analysis of human consciousness.

We have an inner presence that allows us to interact with other real beings within reality, because we *are* reality. (We '*are*' real, no doubt; that doesn't need any demonstration. We *exist*, as Descartes would have said. Understanding means coming to the realisation that *being* real does not mean '*being part*' of reality. We *are*—I repeat—reality. The moment we become self-aware in the good sense, the moment we understand that that 'self' of ours is not really ours, and is not really separate, that is the moment we understand, not with our intellect, but with our whole being.

CONCLUSION

~

I want to go back to something before I wrap this up: curiosity. Human beings are curious; scientists and philosophers are curious. That—many would say—is part of the cognitive component of our consciousness. I don't agree. Purely sentient beings can be curious: cats are curious; many corvids, like crows and magpies, are curious; bears are curious. They are not inquisitive, though. What human beings do that differs from other animals is questioning. No other animal asks questions, or not that we are aware of.

Questioning is one of the expressions of curiosity. It is also an expression of doubt, of perceived possibility, or probability. Our questions have good and not so good qualities. The good qualities are the ones involved in science and philosophy: they are a part of our quest for knowledge. The bad qualities involve doubts about ourselves, fear or fears, anxiety, etc.

Questions in Zen receive no answers (or no logical answers). Koans are famous for being unsolved puzzles. *"What is the sound of one hand clapping?"* *"Why did the Boddhidharma come from the West?"* That is, those questions are not well received. You can ask, but the answer will probably not be to your satisfaction. Zen Masters will tell you that you will not be able to find out about Zen through questioning, because sentience cannot be explained. It can only be demonstrated.

~

If you meditate—as we have seen—if you practice *zazen*, you always surpass the barrier of dualism. Achieving pure concentration means being in touch with everything. Dōgen talked about something called '*the circle of the way*', that is, when you meditate you are using four elements, practice, aspiration, enlightenment, and *satori*. Anyone who practices meditation is enlightened. <u>The good news is that anyone who aspires to become enlightened is already enlightened</u>. There is a unity. Practice and awakening—or '*boddhi*'—are one. Practice, Zen says, is the way of the enlightened ones. Some may not become immediately aware of having achieved *satori*. But it is there the very moment you leave your intellect behind. Even if it's not a lasting experience. That will come too.

And here you see one of the main philosophical differences between Eastern and Western cultures. Inquisitiveness—questioning without acceptance—brings progress and growth. It also brings problems. When you are content, you need no questions. Are further progress and growth necessary? To grow wise you need to learn to accept.

Knowledge and wisdom appear to be antithetical qualities. They have different natures. One comes from cognition and the other one from sentience. Normally, civilised human beings have to choose knowledge in order to function within the collective. Zen tells you you do not need to reject wisdom. You can have everything.

ACKNOWLEDGMENTS

Inés.

www.ingramcontent.com/pod-product-compliance
Lightning Source LLC
Chambersburg PA
CBHW051449290426
44109CB00016B/1683